"Does

and other questions that need to be answered in the Mirror of God's Word."

Grounded in the Word of God and gifted with wisdom, Monica Schmelter invites the reader to engage in the relentless battle between the world's standard of beauty and God's standard of beauty. God's beauty never fades. God sees past all the outward frills and straight into the heart.

Looking into the mirror will never be the same again after reading this interactive book.

-Katherine Degenhardt,
Author and Christian Consultant

Looking in the mirror has always been a struggle. This book has changed my perspective and life. All I can say is thank you to Monica Schmelter for writing *Does This Make Me Look Fat?*

-Samantha

Monica put into words what I have felt in my heart for years—we have to give up the unrealistic, unhealthy standards of worldly beauty and live in what God says. This book is so needed.

-Rosa

This is every woman's battle, and this book is every woman's help in breaking it off with the mirror and scale and moving onto to something far greater and more meaningful.

-Charlene

It's about time we got the focus off our looks, our sizes, and the scales. This book helped me to see the fallacy of striving for the world's standard of beauty. Now that I've finished the book, I see that there is far too much work for me to do in the Kingdom of God to be worried over a five-pound weight gain. I'm going to get busy loving people and reaching out. I'm living to leave a legacy, and I can do that right where I am at my present weight.

-Arline

While reading Monica's latest book, I came to realize that this book was meant for me and for every other girl who has looked in a mirror and said, "I wish my (fill in the blank) was smaller, bigger, or just plain different." This book has practical, biblical truths that can and will help you change the way you view yourself in the mirror and to see your true beauty through God's word and reflect HIS image in the mirror of life—I know it has mine!

-Vickie

Does this Make Me Look Fat?

and other questions that need to be answered in the mirror of God's Word

Monica Schmelter

Copyright © 2013 Monica Schmelter

All rights reserved.

ISBN: 1481806718

ISBN-13: 9781481806718

A Note to Readers

This book is a collection of stories, scriptures, and prayers for and by women and girls. Some of the women are best-selling authors, others are full-time moms, women who work full time, students, unemployed, "underemployed", and the list goes on. The women and girls who contributed stories to this book are African American, Caucasian, Asian, tall, short, petite, athletic, self-confessed couch potatoes—all kinds of Jesus-loving women who have made the commitment to believe that who God says we are in terms of our worth, beauty, and value is far more significant than this world's definition of beauty.

When it comes to our worth and beauty, on some days we feel strong, and on others we feel overwhelmed. So today, we lock arms, join hands, and walk together in faith. In each story, scripture, prayer, and devotion in this book, we provide one another the support and encouragement we all so desperately need when it comes to affirming and understanding our value and true beauty. With that in mind, let's take off our masks, let down our guard, and share our struggles, secrets, and fears, and together, let's hold the Mirror of God's Word and redefine our lives and beauty.

The scriptures in this book are quoted from the New International Version Bible (NIV), the New Living Translation Bible (NLT), the Message Bible (MSG), the King James Bible (KJV), and the Amplified Bible (AMP).

Contents

1. Mirror Mirror on the Wall 1

2. The Carnival "Distorting Mirror" 23

3. The Choice: Hourglass or Magnifying Glass. . .53

4. Whose Mirror Are You Looking Into? 71

5. The Short Sighted Mirror. 81

6. Shattering the World's Mirror. 103

7. The Woman in the Mirror 115

Chapter 1

Mirror, Mirror on the Wall

There is no question that we live in a "touched-up" world. Clearly, crow's feet, muffin tops, and dimpled thighs are not okay in our culture. Models are air-brushed, images are photoshopped, and the message is clear that we are not okay all by ourselves. There is a marketed standard of beauty—an ideal image—and countless girls and women are spending their lives, their money, and their relationships working toward this standard that is simply out of reach for most, and for all, not worth the effort.

Literally billions of dollars a year in the United States alone are spent on the quest to attain beauty. Diets and workout programs are all the rage, and stepping on a little white square can make a girl or woman cry. Even Jesus-loving women find themselves on the perpetual quest to look younger, weigh less, cover up, and hide the flaws.

While looking your best and living a healthy lifestyle is commendable, making your beauty, or perceived lack thereof, the mainstay of your life can be a serious distraction that can leave you on the sidelines of the wonderful life God has planned for you.

This book is designed to give you the biblical tools to lay down the Mirror of this World and its standard of beauty and to pick up the Mirror of God's Word where you will find your true beauty and lasting joy.

With that in mind, let's bravely begin this journey together. It might be difficult at times, but the benefit of living life securely as a daughter of the King is far better than a life of striving for attention, acceptance, and affirmation from those whose opinions are of no consequence.

I know that the worldly standard of beauty for women and girls has been deeply ingrained in our brains, hearts, and spirits. It's everywhere from television to magazines and other people we know and barely know. Our relationship with the mirror usually starts young and lasts a lifetime. We gaze into the mirror with questions and listen intently for answers.

Mirror, mirror on the wall, who is the fairest of them all?

Does this make me look fat?

Am I pretty enough?

Do I need to lose weight?

Is my nose too big?

Would a little Botox help?

Will others find me attractive and/or lovable?

What can I do to improve my appearance?

Insert here whatever question/concern you may have.

One of the many things so important to me is that as women, girls, sisters in Christ, friends, and family, we see the deception that has saturated our planet and penetrated our hearts. This issue of beauty, value, and worth affects everybody, but in this book, we will focus on how it affects women and girls. Even some supermodels struggle with this issue. Many of us look at them and think *if only I could look like her*. All the while, she is working to lose another five pounds or figure out how to make her cheekbones more prominent.

Since I want us to see that we are in this together, I have invited several women to join our conversation throughout this book. I asked them to share their struggles, their victories, and the scriptures that have helped them fight and win the battle of laying down the Mirror of the World and picking up the Mirror of God's Word.

Let's listen as Crystal North shares her heart with us:

As a make-up artist, I have the pleasure of looking into the mirror for at least an hour every single day. I spend that hour perfecting my gift of make-up artistry: covering all the dark circles that last night's lack of sleep left behind, contouring my cheeks so my face will appear thinner, and seeing yesterday's smiles turn into today's crow's feet and laugh lines—oh, the joys of being me! As a woman, oftentimes the image I view in the mirror, which is simply my reflection, determines yesterday's failures, today's successes, and tomorrow's possibilities. I have seen days, weeks, months, and years pass where I have allowed my reflection to define me. It reflected what my oversized hips told me I could never have, where my larger-than-life feet told me I could never go, how my short height defined to me what I could never do, what my distorted vision told me I could never see, and who my seemingly incapable mind told me I could never be. I was the total package for sure!

One morning, during my daily routine of viewing my reflection of imperfections, God told me to take another look at who I was; He reminded me of one of my favorite scriptures:

1 Peter 2:9 (NIV)

But you are a chosen people, a royal priesthood, a holy nation, God's special possession, that you may declare the praises of him who called you out of darkness into his wonderful light.

As I turned my focus from the reflection in my vanity mirror, I saw my reflection in the Word of God. I must say how appropriate it was for Peter to start the scripture off with the word *but*. It is a small conjunction word, yet it has so much meaning because it cancels out everything that has been said previously and puts the focus on the joining statement. With this revelation, I conversed with God and considered how I had been seeing myself versus how Christ sees me. In all of my reasoning, the conversation was something like this:

"I am so overweight." *but* **you are holy.**

"I will never meet *Your* standards, God." **However, I have chosen you.**

"I am such a failure." ***but* you are my special possession.**

That day, I realized the reflection I viewed in the mirror would never and could never define how Christ truly sees me. Realistically, I may have moments when I look at my reflection and sigh at the signs of my aging body, ***but*** when I take another look at me, God reminds me that I am His special possession and I am holy. In that moment, I become perfect for the task at hand, encouraged about the days to come, eager to know Him more, and thankful that He has chosen me.

Prayer

Father God, thank you for choosing me and reminding me that in spite of any imperfections I may see in my mirror, I am your special possession. I pray that you open my eyes so that I will view myself in the way that you truly see me and so that I may continue to declare your praises because you have called me out of darkness into your wonderful light.

In Jesus' Name,

Amen

What can we learn from what Crystal North has to say? Let's take a moment to reflect on her experience with God prompting her to look into the mirror. Might He be saying that to you and me as well? Is it possible that God wants us to look into the mirror again and use His standards to reevaluate what we think we see? Let's take some reflection time and go through the questions below.

Reflection Time

Are there times when you focus solely on your reflection in the mirror? If so, when is that most likely to happen?

Have your perceived flaws ever become larger than life?

Can you open yourself to the truth of God's Word (1 Peter 2:9) and hear what He has to say to you about your value and who He made you to be?

What is God saying to you about your value?

Write 1 Peter 2:9 in your journal or somewhere handy. Speak this scripture aloud. Print and tape this scripture to the mirror where you do your makeup or fix your hair. Immerse yourself in this truth today. **You are God's special possession, and you**

have value that goes beyond your reflection in the mirror.

God's Mirror says many things to us about our worth and beauty. He refers to us as holy, special, and chosen. We counter His Word many times with our insecurities. We look into this world's Mirror and reflect on our "perceived flaws," whether they are a big nose, muffin top, or cellulite. If we're not careful, we can get caught up in the Worldly Mirror. The Bible addresses this:

1 Peter 3:3-4 (NIV)

Your beauty should not come from outward adornment, such as elaborate hairstyles and the wearing of gold jewelry or fine clothes. Rather, it should be that of your inner self, the unfading beauty of a gentle and quiet spirit, which is of great worth in God's sight.

I'm well aware that some people feel this verse means women should not wear jewelry or makeup. That's not what I see as Paul also mentions fine clothes. Certainly, he wasn't saying we shouldn't wear clothes. I believe the heart of what he was saying is that we shouldn't rely on outward things (jewelry, hairstyles, and fine clothing) to be solely responsible for our beauty. For the Christian woman/girl, our beauty comes from a gentle and quiet spirit, on which God places a high value. The world's standard is to measure things by their outward appearance while

God looks on the inside at our hearts. The call and the challenge to each of us as believers in Christ is to hold in higher value what God says than what the world says or tries to require of us.

1 Samuel 16:7 KJV

But the LORD said unto Samuel, "Look not on his countenance or on the height of his stature; because I have refused him: for the LORD seeth not as man seeth; for man looketh on the outward appearance, but the LORD looketh on the heart."

The world and its beauty requirements cross all lines. As women/girls, we're in a similar struggle. Do we live our lives to meet the world's standards, or do we live by every Word that proceeds out of the mouth of God? Let's open our hearts and ears now as we hear from a teenager named Mariah Deese. Even as a teen, Mariah experiences this struggle of what's expected of girls and women, and she shares with us how she fights against this battle:

> When it comes to self-image, it's clear, growing up in this generation, that you are expected to look, dress, and act a certain way. I have come to realize it's impossible to be like those "perfect" models that you see on TV or in magazines. Nobody can be completely flawless on the outside, but God sees

you as flawless on the inside through the finished work of the cross. The "imperfections" that you see on your face/body are not mistakes of any kind. God created you in His own image. God never makes mistakes. So you might ask the question: How do I start to see myself the way God sees me? Here are three great principles that I have learned:

1. Guard Your Friendships – people who do not know who they are can't help you in the process of finding who you are in Christ.

2. Fill your heart with God's Word – as you discover what God says about you, the words of others will hold less value.

3. Guard your heart – This is our God-given assignment. It is not God's responsibility to guard your thoughts about yourself; it is yours.

Proverbs 4:23 (KJV)

Keep thy heart with all diligence; for out of it are the issues of life.

In reality, why should we waste our time trying to be like other people when

MIRROR, MIRROR ON THE WALL

God created us to be unique? We are not cheap duplicate copies of Barbie.

If you spend your time pretending to be someone you're not, who's going to have the time to be you?

Prayer

Dear God,

Teach me today to guard my heart. Father, give me the grace to guard my heart against negative thoughts about myself, or those directed at me from others. I pray today, Father, that my heart will be flooded with your Word about who I am in Christ. Let me walk today in the call that you have for me. Thank you, God, that you have made me unique and that no one can fulfill the role that you assigned to me.

In Jesus' Name,

Amen

It's clear, after reading what Mariah shared, that this battle with the mirror is shared by almost all women and girls. Whether we are fifteen or fifty-five years old, we look into our mirrors intently. We analyze, we criticize, we cover up, and sometimes we cry. What are we going to do about this battle? Should we fight on by covering up and feeling insecure? Should we stay at home when our jeans become too tight? Should we allow the issue of how we think we look to define our life perspective and rule our day-to-day existences? Let's join together right now and consider some important questions. You may want to get your journal out and record your answers for further thought and prayer.

Reflection Time

How can I guard my heart and thoughts against the onslaught of negative concepts such as, *I have to be and look perfect*?

Do I have relationships with true friends that really honor, love, and encourage me, or do I have friends that point out my perceived flaws? If the answer is, "Yes, I have friends that point out my flaws (real or imagined)," what am I willing to do to change this?

Focus today on the scripture out of Proverbs 4:23 on keeping (guarding) your heart. Make a careful mental note (or journal note, too) every time you are tempted to entertain a negative thought and how good it feels when you make the decision to take that thought captive and thus "guard your heart." We can do this. We can do this together. We really can. We Jesus-loving girls can do what God says and guard our hearts in every single area. Don't let your heart be weighed down with other people's (or even your

MIRROR, MIRROR ON THE WALL

own) negative, unrealistic, and insensitive comments or innuendos. We are far too valuable for that!

So far we've heard from Crystal North and Mariah Deese, and they've shared their struggles and victories. Now, Kim Aldrich, speaker, author, and comedian, joins our study as we learn and share together about winning the battle with the mirror.

Here is Kim Aldrich's perspective on being a girl and looking into the mirror:

> Being a girl and looking into a mirror isn't always as fun as advertised. In fact, sometimes it's downright discouraging. "Mirror, mirror, on the wall, who's the fairest of them all?" Are you kidding? How in the world can a flesh-and-blood female live up to the hype of the airbrushed, amped-out, and high-definition world we live in?
>
> For that matter, even "reality" TV stars can't live up to the hype. Imagine how they'd look without a team of make-up artists and professional photographers following them around 24/7 helping them look effortlessly put together. My guess is, even the Kardashians don't look like *The Kardashians* every single minute of the day. Just like the rest of us, they occasionally look into

a mirror and ask, "Who on EARTH is that girl staring back at me, and what would people think of me if they ever saw her?"

I'm wondering what happens to our self-esteem on those "off" days. Are we automatically less lovable on the days when we look less-than-radiant? Does our stock instantly go down the minute our weight, age, or level of bloating goes up, or is there something a little less fragile and a lot more durable that determines our value?

I believe there is.

God's Word says that He will never leave us nor forsake us—never. Not even if we're having a bad skin day, hair day, or face day. He also says He has engraved us on the palms of His hands. And wait until you read this:

2 Corinthians 3:18 (NIV)

And we all, who with unveiled faces contemplate the Lord's glory, are being transformed into his image with ever-increasing glory, which comes from the Lord, who is the Spirit.

For those who know Christ, this is our reality: We're actually getting better looking with each passing day!

As we gaze into Christ's face, His own ageless beauty is reflected in our faces, our hearts, our minds, and our lives. In every way that counts, our beauty is not fluctuating or waning, but actually increasing in glory, day by day, until one day in heaven even our bodies will get the "complete makeover" God has in store for us.

So next time you look at yourself in the mirror, remember this:

Knowing Christ is the best beauty product on the market, and YOU have a lifetime supply!

Prayer

Dear Jesus,

I thank you for the complete makeover that you have in store for me someday. Until that day, I pray, dear Father, that as I gaze into the face of Jesus Christ, His beauty is reflected on an ever-increasing basis in my life. Let my desire for your truth and beauty increase and the desire to achieve the world's standards of beauty grow dim in comparison to who

I really am in you. Let others around me see your beauty and truth in my life.

In Jesus' Name,

Amen.

Reflection Time

Have you considered before that in Christ you have the best beauty product, and that you have a lifetime supply?

Take a moment right now to renew your mind. Carefully consider how in Christ you are actually getting better looking every day! You might say, "No, Monica, that's not true. I'm getting older and heavier," or whatever you think (just fill that in here) but those are thoughts from the world's system and our own carnal minds. In Christ, we are renewed every day. His beauty and glory are reflected in our lives on an increasing basis every single day. That is the whole truth and nothing but the truth. Receive that for yourself today.

When it comes to your battle with the mirror, what do you need to lay down?

Find some examples below:

Unrealistic standard of beauty

Stringent dieting

Excessive workout routines

Restrictive eating

Spending more money than can be reasonably afforded on makeup products, clothing, or cosmetic surgeries

Unhealthy beauty routines

Toxic thoughts such as, *I am ugly, my nose is too big*, and *no one is ever going to want to marry me*

Binging/purging

Weighing in every day (or several times a day)

Purchasing clothes/accessories in order to be accepted and/or noticed

These are just a few examples. There are many, many more. You know the battles that you personally experience. You know your areas of temptation. Take some time to think about what you need to lay down. What areas have you felt the Holy Spirit nudging you in?

I promise you that as you are obedient, God will honor you. Everything you lay down will be replaced with true and lasting value and beauty that no one can ever take from you. Do not be afraid—only believe.

Living a life with God and out of the world's system is the most blessed and beautiful life a girl can live.

Let's share this adventure together. We will lay down the World's Mirror and pick up the Mirror of His Word in which we will see our True Reflection. It's going to be good, girls—it's going to be better than good!

Let's take some time to pause, take a deep breath, and exhale. Out of everything you've read so far, what stands out most to you? Are you making progress in changing your thinking?

Okay, I just heard at least two of you perfectionistic girls like me say, "No, I am not making any progress yet." Let's stop here and hang out a minute. You are making progress. Just the fact that you are still reading this book and studying indicates that progress is underway.

I didn't promise this journey would be quick and/or easy. It's not easy to lay down the Mirror of the World. It requires faith and hard work (sometimes referred to as obedience). So let's join our faith together here and now, and make the choice that we will no longer define our value by the Mirror of the World. We will not believe that our beauty is defined by dimples or lack thereof on our thighs. Laugh lines and crow's feet do not dictate our attitudes or make us beautiful or "old." We no longer accept this world's message and standard of beauty. Perhaps as we make this choice, we will also reject the standards of beauty given to us by our role models. Not everything our families and friends say to us, expect of us, and/or want from us is necessarily the best for us, even if they love us immensely.

In essence, we are rejecting any standard of beauty that does not line up with the Mirror of God's Word. This is our choice. I believe with all my heart that we want to make this choice, and we want to fully obey God's Word and embrace what He says as Truth. From this moment forward, we are hearing God's Word and obeying God's Word. These two actions bring blessings into our lives. We are blessed as we obey.

You might want to make some notes here about God's Truth concerning your beauty and value that you are applying to your life right now. You will carry this progress with you into chapter 2, where we will once again grow and be challenged in faith and beauty together.

Here are some of the truths we have studied in this chapter:

> We are God's special possession.

> Our true value is only realized in Jesus Christ.

> God's Word lasts forever, and our identity is only secure in Him.

We must guard our hearts.

I pray as we journey together that you also will be firmly rooted in these truths. Hold on girls; it's time to progress further on our trip. I know some of you are wondering how long this will take. We are not there yet. We won't be there until we are finally in heaven with Jesus. However, on this side of life's equation, we can join hands, hearts, and in faith, and we can walk together and encourage each other along life's way. We can help each other renew our minds in God's Word. We can together lay down the Mirror of this World and pick up the Mirror of His Word and read it and live it aloud *together*.

In chapter 2, we're hitting it hard. Down with the Lies! Bring on the Truth! Let's bring it on and immerse ourselves in God's Whole Truth and nothing but the Truth! Sound good?

What is the real answer to the question, "Mirror, mirror on the wall, who is the fairest of them all?" The answer is that Jesus is the fairest of them all, and He is madly in love with you and ascribes supreme significance and everlasting beauty to you and your life.

Philippians 2:8-10 (KJV)

And being found in fashion as a man, he humbled himself, and became obedient unto death, even the death of the cross. Wherefore God also hath highly exalted him, and given him a name which is above every name: That

> **at the name of Jesus every knee should bow, of things in heaven, and things in earth, and things under the earth.**

Jesus has the Name above every Name. He is highly exalted by God. Every knee will bow to Him. This means that the Mirror of the World and its unrealistic standards must bow to His supreme Name and greatness. The world is wrong, and Jesus is right. Let's believe this with all our hearts, and live and talk freely because His truth has defeated the Mirror of this World. He has defeated everything that has tried to stand against us.

Chapter 2

The Carnival's Distorting Mirror

I remember clearly that my first trip to a fun house included a stop at the carnival's distorting mirror zone. As I went through the different areas, I was amazed at my reflection in those very weird mirrors. One moment I was tall and skinny. The next minute I was really short and three times as wide. In some of the mirrors, my face was at least four feet wide and my torso very, very small. In this fun house experience, I heard laughs, squeals, and screams of delight and fright as people experienced their distorted reflections. The funniest part of this experience is the knowledge that it's not real. It's distorted, it's make believe, and it's exaggerated, but all the participants know that. That's what makes it funny.

What's not so funny is that for many women and girls, what we see when we look into the mirror is similar to looking into a carnival's distorting mirror. It's as if our reflection is distorted by the lies and unrealistic expectations of this world. On the off chance that you are not familiar with carnival mirrors, here is a simple definition from Wikipedia: "A distorting mirror or carnival mirror is a popular attraction at carnivals and fairs. Instead of a normal plane mirror that reflects a perfect mirror image, distorting mirrors are curved mirrors, often using convex and concave sections to achieve the distorted effect."

This distorted effect is exactly what many women and girls see whenever they look into a regular, normal mirror. Think about the cover of this book for a moment. There is a lovely, attractive woman who looks into the mirror and sees a much larger image than who she is in reality. This distorted effect is different for many women and girls. Some gaze into the mirror to see what they believe is a large nose. Others look into the mirror to see a seemingly flat chest, huge hips, or extra thick waistline. I suppose this list could go on and on, but we all get the point. Our reflection in the mirror can be distorted by unrealistic expectations of the world, our own flesh, and the comments of our friends and family.

Sometimes, our time in the mirror leaves us in tears, makes us want to stay home when we have the

THE CARNIVAL'S DISTORTING MIRROR

opportunity to go out, or it just colors our world in ways that leave us feeling very poorly about ourselves. So what is the answer here? Should we never use the mirror, or should we just ignore what we think we see? Is there a way to stop putting such an emphasis on our outward appearances?

It's important to me that you know that this book is not born from some "I'm above it all" perspective. I've had more than one bad mirror day. I've stayed at home when I felt I looked horrible, I've been reduced to tears when I couldn't cover up a zit, and I've stepped on the scale and wanted to scream and cry loudly. This book is born from many trials, tears, fears, and rejections. My earliest memories include people telling me I was chubby. Then, as if to somehow make up for the inconsiderate nature of their comments, they would say, "But you have such a pretty face."

Early on, most of us learned that in one way or another, we didn't measure up, and thus the visits to the carnival's distorted mirror began. I hope that it's clear that as women/girls from all different walks of life, our struggles with the Mirror of the World telling us that we are in some way unworthy and/or don't measure up is a shared and common experience.

I handled my imagined inferiority with self-loathing, yo-yo dieting, and unrealistic dreams of one day being "*instantly*" thin. I was sure that if I could become a thin girl, my whole life would drastically improve. All I ever managed to do from elementary to high school was to lose a few pounds and then gain back more weight than I originally lost. I never made it "there." I never arrived at "thin."

I endured more "chubby girl" comments than I care to recall. (If you're ever tempted to mention someone's weight in an effort to "help" them, you might want to re-think that.) As a high school student, I heard more "you're not *fat*—you're just big boned" comments than I could count, as if somehow that would make it all better. Then, as an adult, while I was still frustrated with my tendency to pack on the pounds, I felt somewhat more relaxed because many adults go through a middle-age spread. At that point, I at least felt I wasn't the only one. I was miserable, but not so alone in my misery. I still didn't like it, but I didn't feel quite so out of place.

Then at age forty-three, I decided once again to lose weight. This time, I did lose weight. I lost about seventy pounds over the course of a year, and I managed to keep the weight off. Imagine my surprise, though, when all of my problems didn't disappear suddenly. The problem of my clothes growing ever tighter changed to that of clothes becoming looser, but I still struggled with "beauty problems."

Now instead of comments about my growing size, people went on and on as if I was so wonderful for losing weight. I mean, really, you would have thought that I had found the secret to world peace or somehow singlehandedly ended world hunger. It's only weight,

THE CARNIVAL'S DISTORTING MIRROR

people—it's a number on a scale—a size on a pair of jeans. But my goodness, people thought I looked better, people thought I was a better example of a Christian, people thought I was closer to God. People thought stuff and said stuff, and my head and heart were reeling as I tried to somehow soak in and process all of that talk.

These comments set off a completely new struggle for me. When I looked into the mirror, I wondered if I looked as thin as I did the day before. Not only did I wonder about that—people told me about it. They said things like, "Have you lost more weight?" or "Have you gained weight?" and this would happen several times a day. Talk about driving a girl "stinking thinking" crazy! Talk about a trip to the distorting carnival mirror—that was my life every single day, and for me it was definitely not a laughing matter.

It was as if I learned all over again that the Mirror of the World and its lies and deceptions are never ending. The Mirror of the World's lies cross size lines, race lines, gender lines, age lines, and economic lines, and they will suck the joy, beauty, and meaning right out of your life if you don't learn to embrace the Mirror of God's Word as your True North. Without the Mirror of God's Word as our True North we are destined to remain in front of the carnival mirror—complete with its' distortions and twisted perspective of our reflection.

What is a girl/woman to do about this battle with the mirror? Most of us see attaining the world's standards of beauty unrealistic, yet large percentages of women and girls spend all kinds of time, money, and physical, mental, and emotional energy trying to achieve those standards.

One of the first things we can do is just be upfront about the fact that many women and girls face this battle every single day. On the one hand, we may desperately desire to believe God's Word that says unfading beauty equals a pure and gentle spirit, and is of great value in the Lord's sight. On the other hand, we may still have the competing desire to diet stringently, find just the right cover-up, or nip and tuck something that we think is just clearly unacceptable.

Ask God for Help

There is freedom in honesty, and by being honest with God and asking for His help in this area, and sharing our struggles with other faith-filled, God-honoring women, we can find liberty and healing that is not attainable in any other way. One of the reasons that this book is loaded with reflection questions and prayers is so that we can invite God into this delicate and personal area of our lives. It's healing to be honest with God and just say, "I'm tired of the battle of the mirror, and I don't want to stand being judged by the mirror, and look at a twisted distorted view of myself."

As we do this hard work, we also help our daughters and other women and girls win this battle. This is

THE CARNIVAL'S DISTORTING MIRROR

not just about us personally. It's about all women and girls being free in Christ and knowing our value and beauty so that we can touch this world as the unique, valuable people we are. Dare with me to imagine for a moment what our lives and this world would be like if we chose to believe that we are beautiful and made in His image. Might we be able to love others more fully, laugh more loudly, and show more compassion to those who are hurting if we weren't so wrapped up in what sizes we wear?

Reach Out to Trusted Family and Friends for Help

First, we must do the honest work that we need to do before God, and ask for His help. Next, we need to reach out to others we trust who are God-honoring and God-fearing women.

Here is what this kind of help and encouragement can look like:

Several months ago, I had the privilege of interviewing two very talented women for the *Bridges* television show that I host. Both women are authors, speakers, and all-around brilliant, talented, fun-loving, and wonderful women of God. They are Teasi Cannon and Constance Rhodes.

Teasi Cannon authored a hilarious and liberating book entitled *My Big Bottom Blessing: How Hating My Body Led to Loving My Life*. Constance Rhodes is the author of *Life Inside the "Thin" Cage: A Personal Look into the Hidden World of the Chronic Dieter*.

I shared with them in the green room of the station where I work, WHTN, how I struggled with people's comments even after losing weight. I told them how it felt as if I was on a constant roller coaster ride with the various questions people would ask me, such as, "Have you gained weight?" or "Have you lost weight?" all in the same day. Both Constance and Teasi understood and immediately offered me support. I was surprised when they both said how inappropriate those comments were.

Here I had been dealing with comments about my body size since I was a child, and these two very smart, very capable Jesus-loving women both said comments about body size are off limits. That had never occurred to me before. I know that might sound crazy to you, but here's a great big dose of truth: When we hear a lie over and over, the lie starts to sound true, or at least okay. That's what happened to me. I heard people talk about my weight so much that I just came to accept it as normal and that it was my job to deal with it.

It was as if day after day, people held up the Mirror of the World and said in various ways, "Monica, you don't measure up," or "You're doing good today—keep it up." I had come to the place where I just endured the comments and suffered in silence. The words of Teasi and Constance brought healing to my life. I felt much better after my conversation with them. It felt as if a huge burden had been lifted—I felt free. In fact, I started feeling freer each day after I spoke with them.

My honest conversation with them allowed me to see God's truth in a new way. I started to see myself in the Mirror of God's Word—beautiful and holy—and that a man's, or a woman's comments, no matter how well intended or not, are not the scale by which I should determine my value.

In fact, I got so inspired after my conversation with them that I started setting boundaries with people who made comments about my weight/body size. Boundaries come in all shapes and sizes, and we can all pick how, when, and what we want to set as our limits. I'll just give you a few examples so you'll have a clearer idea of what I'm discussing.

When comments were made by complete strangers or people who are new acquaintances, I just quietly held up my shield of faith and said to myself, *I will not let this compliment or this fiery dart penetrate my life or spirit. This is an unwanted, unsolicited comment about something very personal, and I choose in Jesus' Name to reject it.*

We have power to reject others' comments whether they are well intended or not. I did not have to be rude or explain to them where I was coming from—some of these people have been total strangers to me, and I don't have a relationship with them where I can comfortably ask for more information to obtain clarity. I just held up my shield of faith and extinguished those fiery darts, and then I did not expend any emotional energy trying to figure out what they meant. Now

DOES THIS MAKE ME LOOK FAT?

that's true freedom, when we don't have to spend our time and emotional energy analyzing what others say. Just think about how much time you've spent wondering what so-and-so meant when she said such-and-such.

In other cases, where I have had a relationship with the person, I started saying gently, "I prefer you not mention my weight or size—it's off limits," and then I would laugh hysterically. If you know me well enough, or have ever seen me on television, then you know I have a most distinctive and obnoxious laugh (it's not on purpose; it's just an all-natural distinctive, obnoxious-sounding laugh). It's one of those deep loud laughs, and once I start, I usually cannot stop. My laugh can definitely change the course of a conversation, so I use it to my full advantage in warding off unwanted comments about my weight and physical appearance.

My hope and my prayer for you as we hang out together, study, and pray through this book is that we will help one another. My prayer is that we will reach out and encourage one another through God's Word to lay down the lies, and then pick up and embrace the truth.

The battle with the mirror is nothing new. Frequent visits to the carnival mirror are not new or unique either. This has been going on for years. It's something most women and girls accept without challenge. We see the truth of God's Word, and yet our hearts are filled with the desire to live up to the world's standards. The Bible makes it clear that no man or woman can serve two masters, and yet on some level, many of us women are trying to do just that despite the difficulty and pain it brings us. My prayer for all of us is that we'll turn the tide and change the course of our lives so that this self-inflicted negativity no longer causes us pain or strips us of our God-given beauty and value.

There are women right now on stringent diets, borrowing money for expensive surgeries, completing excessive workout routines, cutting, binging, giving themselves over to promiscuous behavior, and wearing provocative clothing, all in the hopes of feeling loved, accepted, valued, wanted, and attractive.

In our day-to-day lives, the trips to the carnival mirror are not funny. That distorted image we see when we put on a new outfit or work to cover up a blemish can cause a depth of anguish that feels similar to falling into a bottomless pit.

Ashley Ramps is going to join us to talk about something that I think is paramount to our success. Ashley is a country Christian singer/songwriter, worship leader, television host, and most importantly, one very smart and beautiful young woman.

Here is what Ashley has to say about breaking up with the mirror:

Breaking Up with the Mirror

Have you ever had plans that you were so excited about and looked forward to so much? You know the kind of plans: You're going shopping for a brand new outfit to wear, and you're so excited to wear your new clothes that you can't sleep the night before your big day. Only, you wake up the day of your big plans and find that you're having what we women like to call a "fat day." All of a sudden, the cute outfit we just bought is not so cute. Even though we just tried it on the night before, today we are disgustingly fat, and the outfit looks terrible!

We just need to pause during these moments of deep, dark crisis in our lives and think logically for a moment. When was the last time you actually gained five pounds overnight? We may feel like we have, and we may let our feelings convince our eyes that we have, but realistically, it is all in our head.

We need to come to a point where we are sick and tired of letting the mirror control and ruin our lives. The mirror, when we allow it, has the power to determine the outcome and mood of our days. Just like an unhealthy

THE CARNIVAL'S DISTORTING MIRROR

relationship, we need to break up with the mirror.

When we let the truth sink in that God made each of us uniquely beautiful, it has the power to change our lives. Do you realize that you are the only one who possesses YOUR beauty in this world? It is a beauty that God created for the sole purpose of bringing glory to Him. Why do we constantly tear ourselves apart, then? Why is our standard some photoshopped model instead of the standard of beauty that God created us for?

1 Peter 3:4 (NLT)

You should clothe yourselves instead with the beauty that comes from within, the unfading beauty of a gentle and quiet spirit, which is so precious to God.

We as Christian women are the examples to young girls. We have the ability to set a new standard of beauty. While we are tearing ourselves to pieces about how we look, girls as young as five think they are fat, and girls as young as seven develop eating disorders. This breaks my heart.

Just like you would end that unhealthy relationship you have been holding on to, break it off with your mirror. Look into the mirror, as hard as it may be, and tell yourself, "I am beautiful." Those are POWERFUL words, and when we believe them about ourselves, we are able to let the beauty that God uniquely gave each of us radiate for Him. Think of the freedom we can walk in when our confidence is in the Lord and not the mirror.

Ashley has shared how accepting our culture's standard of beauty as our personal truth may leave us feeling insecure, anxious, and controlled by the mirror. This kind of "societal pressure" can cause us to entertain totally illogical thoughts. This struggle with the carnival mirror may sideline you from fully participating in the abundant life God desires for you. After all, if our culture's standard of beauty has been internalized as the truth, then you may be tempted to sit life out if your jeans are too tight rather than get out there and enjoy it to the fullest. Are you willing to consider taking the challenge that Ashley just laid out? Are you willing to break up with the mirror?

Are you willing to be an example to young girls and set a new standard of beauty? As women, we should be willing to turn the tide on this unrealistic craze for beauty that has so affected our culture that even five-year-olds think they are fat and that seven-year-olds develop eating disorders.

THE CARNIVAL'S DISTORTING MIRROR

These are just a couple of examples of how the world's standards torment us. Our culture is filled with women and girls who are sitting on the sidelines crying their eyes out because they think their eyes aren't pretty, their thighs have too much cellulite, and their abdomens are covered with stretch marks. Seriously, are we going to let this continue without a fight? Can we hear Ashley's heart today and say, "I refuse to accept as my standard a photoshopped model rather than the standard of beauty that God has given to me"?

Hopefully, we are closer to shattering the lie of the distorted carnival mirror as we continue on this journey of laying down the mirror of the world and picking up the Mirror of God's Word as our only true standard of value and beauty.

In the next section, I've changed the names to protect the privacy of the women and girls who have been so brave and honest in sharing some of their struggles with beauty. Here is a sample email that I received:

> Dear Monica,
>
> My whole life has been tainted by an image of unattainable beauty. I have starved myself, gone to numerous dermatologists, filed down my own teeth, and purchased tons of beauty products that all promised me perfection. My friends and family

plead with me to stop, stating that I am blowing everything way out of proportion. What can I do to stop this chase for unattainable beauty?

Help!

Signed,

Anonymous woman under thirty years old who is a wife and mother

What is the answer to this woman's cry for help? Is it one easy prayer? Is it this seemingly pat and curt answer: All of us are beautiful and made in the image of God. That's true, you know; all of us are beautiful and made in the image of God. It's also true that all of us who have spent any time in front of the mirror of our culture have seen that distorted carnival image at least once, and it has fooled us into believing that we are lacking and need to improve.

The challenge here, my dear sisters and friends, is to learn to put down our culture's mirror and pick up the Mirror of God's Word. We need to learn to prioritize His voice and understand that what He says about us is more valuable and authentic than what this world says. This is no easy challenge, but it can be done—and it must be done.

This world is not going to stop with its messages to us. This world is going to continue in ever-increasing measures to sell us beauty products, Botox, liposuc-

38

tion, and messages of our imperfection. I would not purport to tell anyone what products or procedures to buy or not buy. Those are an individual's choices. I suggest that in order to maintain your sanity, your peace, and the complete enjoyment of your life, do not buy into the lie that your beauty and worth are based solely on your reflection in the mirror, and certainly not in the reflection of the carnival mirror's distorted image.

We are more than our reflections in the mirror. We are more than the size of our jeans. Our value and worth is **not** measured on the bathroom scale or in our Body Mass Index (BMI). Whether you can run a marathon or a corporation is not the point. Your life is designed by a supernatural, omniscient, omnipresent Holy God and Heavenly Father, and He says that you have great value. He says that He has more thoughts toward you than the grains of sand on the seashore.

Psalm 139:17-19 (NLT)

How precious are your thoughts about me, O God. They cannot be numbered! I can't even count them; they outnumber the grains of sand! And when I wake up, you are still with me!

His is the voice that we need to hear first and most loudly in our lives. We need to do this for the daughters of future generations, for our daughters, and for ourselves. We are losing a generation of young, and not so young, women to anorexia, bulimia, cutting, and sexual promiscuity. These women have bought the lie that their beauty and worth are measured by the reflection in the mirror and/or the number on a scale.

Certainly, the messages of the media have played a role in this deception. However, we cannot blame it all on the media. Many grown adult women—mothers, grandmothers, aunts, and sisters—have also participated in perpetuating this deception, even if it has been done unknowingly or unwittingly. After all, these women and girls have seen us sigh in despair at our reflection in the mirror. They have heard our conversations about being "too fat," and they have watched us struggle with the scale. They have seen us stay home because *we can't find anything to wear*"! They have seen us pay outrageous sums of money for quick weight-loss programs, Botox, and tummy tucks. Please understand that I am *not* criticizing you if you've done any or all of these. It's just that the overriding message for women has been that our own God-given beauty is not enough; that somehow we must pay, strive, strain, and starve to attain to some objective standard of beauty and perfection that is always just a few pounds, workouts, or a procedure away. Somehow, we have linked this with being liked, accepted, popular, and in some cases, even being better examples as Christians.

So what should we do about this dilemma? We should expose the lie. Let's tell the truth. Perhaps we've been far too concerned with our physical appearance. Perhaps today is the day to turn this tide. Perhaps today is the day to put down the world's mirror —its carnival distorting properties and all—and pick up the Mirror of God's Word and redefine our lives, value, and beauty.

Counselor Maggie Warren joins us now as we journey forward in our search for permanent and lasting truth:

How can we allow the Lord to use us to set the captives free? This requires seeking freedom in our own lives. I found out early in my walk with the Lord that I could not give away what I do not possess. Because I was radically saved, I had a good understanding of salvation and led many people to the Lord. However, walking out my freedom was not quite so easy. It was a journey. Truly, all believers have to travel deeper in fellowship with the Lord to see themselves the way God sees them, and not see the distorted view that society sees, that others see, or even that our own twisted perspective thinks we see.

We are daughters of the King and we can no longer hold on to all of the distorted thought patterns of how we see others or ourselves. The fruits of not seeing ourselves as God sees us are the countless, harassing thoughts from the enemy as well as the low self-esteem we struggle with. The Lord is standing with arms wide open. He wants to embrace us and heal us from the inside out. We are like onions with layers of pain and fear that the Lord wants to peel away. When we allow Him to do this, the light that shines through us will radiate onto a hurting world, and we will definitely have something to give away—the Father's love, unhindered and flowing freely through us to a lost and dying world.

Isaiah 61:1 (NIV)

The Spirit of the Sovereign Lord is on me because the Lord has anointed me to preach good news to the poor. He has sent me to bind up the brokenhearted, to proclaim freedom for the captives and release from darkness for the prisoners.

Prayer

Father, let us not get in the way of doing your will on the earth. We thank you, that you have allowed us to represent you. Therefore, we ask that you would

THE CARNIVAL'S DISTORTING MIRROR

wash our minds of the distorted view of ourselves. Replace the distortion with what you see—how you look at us. Give us boldness! Make us clean, from the inside out. Help us to be more like You in all we say and do.

In Jesus' Name,

Amen

As we said that Amen together, God began immediately to answer and work in our lives. As we are willing to yield to Him, He is molding and shaping us for His glory. He is replacing our distorted perception of what we look like and who we are with the ability to see who we are in Christ. Just as Maggie said, we are daughters of the King, and as such, we cannot hold on to distorted thought patterns of others and of ourselves.

One of the major components we miss when gazing into the distorted carnival mirror is that there are other people on this planet besides us. It's hard to think about that when our brand new outfit that was so cute the day before now looks too tight. In these moments, our vision is distorted, and we think only about ourselves—how we look, how we feel, and how we should stay at home and pull the covers up over our head. This distorted view of ourselves causes us to miss the opportunity to reach the hurting woman at work or in our small care groups at church.

Most of us have spent some time wanting to make a difference for God's Kingdom. We've really wanted to love and serve others. We've wanted to reach out with grace, prayer, love, and mercy. The only problem is that sometimes that desire is cut short because we're in the middle of our crisis with the mirror or scale. It's hard to think in God's terms about our family member who's sick, or our annoying co-worker, when we are busy crying our eyes out because something is wrong with our bathroom scale. We try stepping on the scale more lightly, and we move the scale across to the other side of the room. We remove a layer of clothing—anything to change the readout on the scale—all the while, there are people around us who need our help, prayer, and friendship.

Do you see the deception of the distorted carnival mirror? It takes what is there and twists it to something contorted and out of sorts. In the meantime, real life is happening all around us, but we are too self-involved to notice, or perhaps even to care.

There is a whole world out there that desperately needs the good news that we have. I don't say that to make you feel guilty about taking time for good grooming, working out, and/or eating or preparing healthy food. The Bible does not teach us – I repeat the Bible does not teach us to ignore ourselves and put others first all the time. What the Bible does teach us is what Maggie said: "We are to relate to others and ourselves as daughters of the King". Seeing ourselves in the reality of this role makes those distorted, nega-

44

THE CARNIVAL'S DISTORTING MIRROR

tive thoughts flee. As those thoughts dissipate, we become free and can represent Christ with purity and beauty. In doing so, we experience His love, power, and freedom, first for ourselves, and then as we reach out to others.

Reflection Time

Do you see yourself as a Daughter of the King?

If not, how might this approach change things?

Are you willing to let down your guard and allow God to peel those layers back?

Are you starting to see how laying down the carnival mirror is the key to your personal freedom and the fulfillment of God's plan for you to reach out to others?

Will you let Him wash your distorted view of who you are and what you look like?

As we allow Him to wash our minds of any distortions regarding our value and/or looks, it's important to understand that one of the ways we cooperate with this process is to open our lives and ourselves to the truth of God's Word and the wise counsel of other women who are successfully fighting this battle. By success, I do not mean that we never again think, *Oh my goodness, I am so fat*. I mean that when/if these negative thoughts come, we take them captive and make them obedient to Christ. We won't get there

45

until heaven. Until then, we rely on Him and stay in fellowship with others who can help us to see the truth about who we are.

At this point, let's welcome Kathy Chapman-Sharp to our conversation. She's an author and speaker who has worked on the mission field. She's a wife, a mom, and a friend—she's a real person just like you and me. She's someone who is allowing the truth to set her free. Open your ears and hearts to what she has to say. Meet Five Foot Nothing Kathy Chapman-Sharp.

> When my daughter Rebekah was eight years old, she told me the story of Amy Carmichael, an Irish woman who followed God to India where she eventually founded a mission and orphanage in Dohnavur. As a young child, Amy often wished that her eyes were blue like her little brother's rather than brown. In fact, at night before going to bed, she would often pray that Jesus would change her eye color. Jumping out of bed in the morning, Amy would run to her mirror to see her new blue eyes, and was always disappointed when her prayers had not been answered.
>
> When God called her to minister in India, Amy finally realized God's wisdom in giving her brown eyes. Often criticized by colleagues for her unorthodox

methods, she wore Indian dress and dyed her light skin with strong, dark coffee. She often traveled hundreds of miles on India's hot dusty roads to save a child from the life of being a temple servant, and because Amy Carmichael had brown eyes, she was able to gain the acceptance of the Indian people and allowed to enter the temples where she rescued hundreds of children.

Wow! I think God knew what He was doing when He gave Amy Carmichael brown eyes! I can't say that I've ever wanted blue eyes. Mine are dark brown, and I've always been partial to them. My nemesis has always been my height. I topped out at sixty inches in junior high, which I affectionately dubbed "five foot nothing." "Stand up, Kathy," they would often say. "I am," I would answer. I've never enjoyed being short, but like Amy, I've learned that God accounts for every detail of our creation in His work.

Take a long look at yourself in the mirror. You may not be happy about some things, but it's important to realize that God created you the way He did for His greater purpose. Yes, it's easy to obsess about weight or the fact that we don't look like a supermodel. It's even easier to get sidetracked from God's truth and start thinking that physical appearance is the most important quality to have, or that our intelligence, talents, and achievements can bring us power and wealth.

However, realize this: Everything about you was created to bring honor and glory to God—everything. That means our self-worth is based in Christ and His magnificent love for us! Life in Christ is deeper than eye color, weight, height, and physical beauty. Because of that, we don't have to dwell on what we perceive to be imperfections—rather, we can look forward to discovering the life and ministry that God has uniquely crafted for us!

Psalms 139:14 (HCSB)

I will praise you because I have been remarkably and wonderfully made.

Dear Jesus,

I thank you that I am fearfully and wonderfully made. I thank you that you have planned every detail of my life down to my eye color. You know best, Father, and I yield to you. I surrender to who you are and to your plan. Father, utilize my life as an instrument for your purposes. I pray I will not be distracted by what I think I lack, and I will not waste time being prideful, but rather, I pray that each moment of my life is spent giving you glory so that the others around me will see your beauty in my life.

In Jesus' Name,

Amen

Reflection Time

Have you reflected on the fact that everything about you, down to your eye color, was given to you by God so that you might bring Him glory?

Have you ever allowed yourself to really believe that our Father knows best?

Take some time right now to think about how you are fearfully and wonderfully made. The next time you look into the mirror and are tempted to find the flaws, or the next time someone makes what sounds like a negative assessment of your appearance, take a moment to *stop* and remember that you are fearfully and wonderfully made.

This is part of taking every thought captive and making it obedient to Christ. We can do this, girls. We can do this. We can win this war by focusing on Him and believing that what He says about us is true.

Quit "Buying" the Lie

Trips to the distorted carnival mirror twist our thinking and intensify our emotions. These trips to the mirror usually center on finding the flaw and going to any extreme to "fix" or cover up that flaw. What if instead of that you took Kathy Chapman-Sharp's word to heart and decided that everything—yes *everything* about us was created to bring glory and honor to God. This will change things. We will no longer spend time covering up, fixing, and crying about what we think shouldn't be there. We just need to be brave enough and sick enough of pulling, primping, twisting, and covering up that we just let go and believe God is right and that the world is wrong.

Who said that an oval is the ideal facial shape? Who said that long lean legs are most attractive? Who said that small noses are superior to larger ones? Who exactly made the brilliant decision that being size zero was the right size for every woman on planet earth? Imperfect people just like us made those decisions. Over the years, these people have changed their minds about beauty on several occasions. It used to be that larger women with well-rounded abdomens and curvy thighs were considered the epitome of beauty. Then many years later, there was Marilyn Monroe, and then after that, there was Twiggy.

I point this out only to demonstrate the fragile and ever-changing nature of beauty standards. I can't tell you how many times I've thought, *If I only had been born X number of years ago—I would have met the world's standards!* But the reality is that we were all born exactly when God ordained us to be. He formed us and shaped

THE CARNIVAL'S DISTORTING MIRROR

us and made us in His image. That alone trumps any manmade standard. As Kathy Chapman-Sharp pointed out, we are fearfully made, and thus we will praise Him.

Take some time right now to praise Him. Thank Him for who you are. Thank you for your unique life and beauty. Thank Him for your intrinsic value. Tell Him how pleased you are that He put you on this earth at this time and that you graciously accept His plan and purpose for your life.

Break up with the Mirror

I wish we could all be in the same room together right now. I'd like to hear that sound of us shattering the carnival's distorted mirror and replacing it with the Truth of God's Word. I'd like to see the smiles on all of our faces as we praise Him for how fearfully and wonderfully He made us. I'd like to hear the stories of how you're better able to reach out to others and love them unconditionally because you're at a healthier place in terms of understanding and reflecting your God-given beauty and value. We have nothing to lose but the enemy's distortions of who we are, and we have everything to gain by living in freedom as daughters of the King.

It's over as of today—we are breaking up with the Mirror!

51

Chapter 3

The Choice: Hourglass or Magnifying Glass

Our lives are filled with choices. God has given each of us a free will, and He lets us choose everything from whether we will serve Him to whether we want to go to college. Obviously, some of our decisions have greater impact and consequences than others, but they are still our decisions. When it comes right down to it, we all have the choice as women and girls to live like an hourglass or a magnifying glass. The choice is all ours, and so are the benefits and consequences.

If the choice to be an hourglass or magnifying glass belongs to us, it would seem important to understand the distinctions. Our lives are gifts from God, and yet He allows us to make our own choices and determine how we'll spend our time and lives. I'm pleased right now to introduce you again to author and speaker Teasi Cannon.

Teasi has had a tremendous influence on my life, though I don't know her very well. I've read her book, and I've had her on *Bridges* several times. Her unique perspective has encouraged me greatly. I know she will have a significant influence on how you think about your value and beauty as a woman and as a daughter of the King.

Let's listen as Teasi shares her heart with us:

1 Corinthians 6:20 (KJV)

For you were bought at a price; therefore glorify God in your body and in your spirit, which are God's.

Beauty is important; there is no mistaking that, but it is possible to make a mistake when we decide whose beauty is most important: God's or ours.

I realize we might not always be consciously aware of it, but the decision really comes down to this: Do you want to be an hourglass or a magnifying glass?

As an hourglass, we will live each day as if our beauty is most important. Anything that tells us we're not beautiful enough has the potential to devastate us.

We will be desperate to do all we can to maximize our own beauty. We might spend money we don't have on clothes, makeup, or cosmetic procedures. We might work our bodies to exhaustion in an attempt to be perfectly firm, toned, and shaped—like an hourglass. Thoughts of our own beauty, whether good or bad, will occupy our minds regularly.

As a magnifying glass, we will live each day as if God's beauty is most important. Anything that tells us God is not beautiful will devastate us, and we will strive to make decisions that glorify Him. In the Greek, the word glorify from 1 Corinthians 6:20 means "to magnify." Are we living our lives in such a way that when people look at us, they see the beauty of the Lord more clearly? If so, we're being a magnifying glass.

We must ask ourselves this question: *When people look at me, do I want them to be amazed with my beauty or with God's?*

There is nothing wrong with wanting to look our best and take care of ourselves, but let's determine together to be magnifying glasses for our Lord.

Dear Jesus,

Please help me to see from your perspective whether I am an hourglass or a magnifying glass. Father, by the power of your Holy Spirit, help me to see any blind spots that I may have. When people look at me, I want them to be amazed with your beauty and goodness. Show me, Father, how to be a reflection of your goodness and beauty every single day and in every single situation.

In Jesus' Name,

Amen

Reflection Time

In what ways are my thoughts like an hourglass or a magnifying glass?

Am I willing to allow my life to become a magnifying glass?

Am I willing to lay down my hourglass? Please relax, this does *not* mean that you will stop showering, putting on make- up or even working out. (This means that outward beauty and the search for thereof, does not occupy our minds, our time, our lives, and our wallets for the majority of our existence, not that we should stop doing things we enjoy, such as putting on makeup or working out.)

When people look at me, are they amazed with God's beauty?

List two things that will help you transition to becoming a magnifying glass.

We can do this sisters and friends. We can join in faith, and we can pray and work toward becoming magnifying glasses for our Lord. Truly, I want people to be amazed with God's beauty when they see and interact with me. In all likelihood, that's what you want, too. Sometimes we just need a gentle nudge to tell us to stop thinking as an hourglass and begin thinking as a magnifying glass. Consider this your little nudge, dear sisters and friends.

As we receive and heed that little nudge, we will move together toward becoming a magnifying glass content to allow God's beauty to be reflected in our everyday lives. Becoming that magnifying glass requires commitment on our part. One of the main commitments is to believe and obey God's Word above all else. This means that rather than desiring attention for our natural beauty—the compliments, adoration, and admiration—we are pleased to show forth God's grace and beauty in our character with such things as our gentleness, love, patience, honesty, and truth. In order to be a magnifying glass, we truly have to live as if the character of Christ is far more significant than the readout on our bathroom scale.

At this juncture, I am inviting Katie Cloyd to join our conversation. Katie is a wife, a brand new mom, an artist, and author of the book titled *Being the Fat Girl: My True Life Story from Heartache to Triumph*. I met Katie when she was single, and I was so impressed with her handle on life and her ability to see that when it comes to a woman's true beauty and value, the world is just plain blind.

Let's listen as Katie shares her heart with us:

I Timothy 4:8 (NIV)

For physical training is of some value, but godliness has value for all things, holding promise for both the present life and the life to come.

For as long as I can remember, I have been fighting a war with my weight, and to be honest, I have not yet won. As an overweight woman, I feel a daily pressure to change everything about my body before I can be perceived as beautiful. Despite having a life that is overflowing with love and blessings and answered prayers, I sometimes find myself refusing to be content because I am so obsessed with what other people think about how I look.

In my quest to lose weight, I have met some success. I hope that through hard work I will one day reach a healthy weight for my body. I know it is important to work hard to get this temple of the Most High God into a healthier condition.

But it is far more important for me to remember that my first obligation is to godliness, and that learning to love like Jesus is my highest goal. Even today, while the mirror shows me an image I am not always happy to see, there is a Holy One who looks at me and sees exactly how beautiful I am. He sees the best parts of me: my great successes. He sees the parts of my heart that are tender toward His children. He sees the most gentle and quiet parts of my spirit where true beauty lives. This beauty will live on forever, and it is on this beauty that I must work.

I love it when I hear Katie say, "It is this beauty (the gentle and quiet parts of my spirit) that will live on forever, and it is on this beauty that I must work." Because you see, my dear friends and sisters, this is what matters forever. The workouts we endure do some good. The benefits of working out are many, though they don't last forever. Therefore, in living our lives and setting our priorities, we must ask ourselves what would rank number one on our priority list: working out or working on having a gentle and quiet spirit. This is a decision that only we can make.

It's totally our choice. We can plug away torn between the promise of worldly beauty, the promise of our next diet or diligent workout, or we can humbly

DOES THIS MAKE ME LOOK FAT?

yield to our Father and ask Him to make us gentle and pure-hearted women. This kind of beauty doesn't fade with time, age, or life experience. If we're wise, we'll make the decision that Katie has made. We'll make the decision to be a magnifying glass for the Lord and allow the rest of the things in our lives to take lesser priority.

It's amazing, how much time, emotional energy, thought, and finances we put toward becoming an hourglass when our flesh is clearly fading away. This body and our outer beauty that demands so much attention and causes so much angst are here today and gone tomorrow. How sad really to allow something that is passing away to occupy so much time, focus, and money.

That's one of the reasons this journey is so important. It's not just another fad or trend. This is truth. This is what's important to God. Our inner selves are being renewed every day, and we have the ability to demonstrate to the world the amazing beauty and love of our God.

Have you made your choice yet? Will you be a magnifying glass or an hourglass? Let's be brave enough in Christ to stand up straight and tall and say, "I'm not buying the lie anymore!" I won't put a higher priority on covering up crow's feet than I will on allowing God's character to be formed in me. Are you ready to agree with me that we will be magnifying glasses?

We will show people the beauty of our Lord. We will show people how amazing His love and grace are when we open our hearts and lives to Him, but doing this requires faith and trust. Even the decision to become a magnifying glass rather than an hourglass requires faith and trust. *Well, how can we do that?* you might ask. It's a fair question. Here on earth we are surrounded by a world that is obsessed with physical beauty. Just watch television for thirty minutes. You'll see the world's most beautiful people on the shows and commercials. Just read a magazine, most of the women in those publications are very tall and thin. They do not at all represent the average woman (whatever it is that "average" means).

Both women and men (and young girls too) have been sold a bill of goods about what's expected and *"beautiful"*. Then, at some point, we realize, *hey, this is craziness!* This is *"insane"* to spend inordinate amounts of time and money seeking ways to be more beautiful, and following unhealthy eating plans just to achieve the perfect measure of thinness. What is it that we can do to change this?

Decide to Lay Down the Mirror of the World

Well, as you might have guessed, there is no simple program to overcome the battle with the world's mirror. There are, however, some keys to freedom, which begin with our decision to lay down the mirror of the world and embrace the Mirror of God's Word. When it comes to the Mirror of God's Word, we can fully rely on this truth: God values us. God has given us value

DOES THIS MAKE ME LOOK FAT?

through His Son Jesus Christ. This fact makes all the difference.

This journey is not about you *trying hard* to get over your preoccupation with looking better, being the most beautiful woman in the room, or changing the size of your nose and/or anything else that might be plaguing you. This journey is about recognizing that God places a huge value on us and has given us His only Son, Jesus Christ, so that we can be restored and whole in every area of our lives.

In this world, our value is contingent on who we are—our material possessions and physical looks, but with our heavenly Father, our value is found in His Son Jesus Christ. We can walk this journey and live in this world but not be "of" this world. We start on that road to freedom by acknowledging and receiving that God values us.

Right now, you will meet my friend Janet McClung. She's a wife, mom, businesswoman, pastor's wife, mentor, prayer partner, and all around fun-loving person. Janet is going to share with us how God's value on our lives makes all the difference. Take it away, Janet!

> Someone once gave me a little square potting cup of dirt. In that dirt was a green plant with a card attached. The plant was an ivy cutting, and the card read, "I just want you to know that I Value You."

Since that time, I've never been able to get away from the thought that no matter what my life may look like to me and maybe even others—I may feel like that square cup of dirt—but up from the dirt, God has designed a beautiful life for me that He values.

Situations arise in our lives that try to make us doubt our self-worth or ourselves. Sometimes we listen to people around us speaking negatively or to a culture that tells us and shows us that we must be, must look, and must act a certain way to be accepted and loved. Even some choices we make can seemingly put us on a road to having no sense of value. Or you may look into a mirror and see yourself as just ordinary.

God does not see us as worthless, hopeless, or useless, He sees us as His Great Treasure. God wants us to know that He values us so much that He gave His only begotten Son so that we might have everlasting life. He paid the ultimate sacrifice just so we would know He values us.

When we are experiencing the pressures of this world, if we will take a few quiet moments, He will whisper to us and remind us just how important we are to Him. We can hear Him say, "My daughter, I Value You!"

God says, "I Value You so much that I will never leave you, and I will never forsake you. On the highest mountaintop and even in your darkest valley, I will always be with you, my daughter, because I Value You!"

So today and every day we can look into that mirror, and say, "God values me!"

1 Corinthians 6:19-20 (KJV)

What? Know ye not that your body is the temple of the Holy Ghost which is in you, which ye have of God, and ye are not your own? For ye are bought with a price: therefore glorify God in your body, and in your spirit, which are God's.

Dear Jesus,

Thank You Jesus, that You value me! Thank You that you designed and created my life for Your purpose. You have made me valuable in Christ, and have blessed me so that I can make a difference for good in this world. Give me eyes to see and a heart to understand and obey today.

In Jesus' Name,

Amen

Reflection Time

Replace Each Lie with the Truth

You are God's great treasure. You are His precious possession. Ask God to show you every place in your life where you may have believed a lie about your value.

Replace each of those lies with His truth. Select two to three verses and commit them to memory to remind yourself that He Values You.

You are His treasure, and He has committed Himself to you. You are not alone in trying to live this life. You are **not** dependent on other people's opinions or standards of beauty. He Values You.

The value that He places on you gives you the freedom and supernatural power to lay down the desire to be an hourglass and instead become a magnifying glass for His glory. I see so many women and girls these days, whether I am at church or at the mall, who seem to be striving to be an hourglass. That is, they appear to be dressed to draw attention to themselves.

Modesty

Clearly, a wide variety of attire that our culture finds acceptable is nothing more than seductive or provocative. Before you stop reading or become frustrated, please hear my heart here. God is *not* against beauty—He is the Author of beauty. God is not against fun colors and patterns—just look outside at the flowers, trees, and wildlife. What a wide array of beautiful diversity He placed in the natural world! God created femininity. God gave women and girls the desire to look pretty, but the world's carnival mirror has distorted that from "pretty" to "sexy."

In our culture, innocent young girls are encouraged and even pressured to look "sexy" rather than pretty. Much of that may come from television and the media, but not all of it. I've noticed a great number of grown women, even Christian women, who have bought the lie of the world's distorting mirror. Rather than drawing their beauty from a pure and gentle spirit, women are donning the deepest V-Neck shirt, the shortest skirt, and the tightest pants they can find in a vain effort to gain attention and affirmation.

I won't argue that dressing in the above manner won't get you noticed. It will. Whether a Christian woman wants this kind of attention is another subject entirely. On the one hand, as Jesus-loving girls, we want to be appreciated, affirmed, and loved for who we are, and that's a godly desire. Yet at the same time, we may have the competing interest to be an

THE CHOICE: HOURGLASS OR MAGNIFYING GLASS

"hourglass" and thus be noticed. This kind of attention is empty, as its validation is based solely on how we look. It's never enough. After all, there is always someone younger, thinner, prettier, more seductive looking, and readily available. Deep within our heart of hearts, we know because we're made in God's image that unconditional, agape love is the answer to every woman's heart and cry for a relationship. You just can't get that by dressing to be an "hourglass." That kind of attention and validation is vain, empty, and carnal.

So, what are we to do in this battle of the hourglass versus the magnifying glass? It's up to us to stand against this trend in our culture and even in our churches. Again, I want to make it clear that I am not suggesting you put away your makeup or that you stop shopping for cute clothes. In fact, if we ever get a chance to meet in person, it would be fun to share makeup techniques, talk fashion, and go shopping. I'm always looking for good bargains, too. What I am talking about is that as Jesus-loving women, we need lose the desire to dress for attention. We need to give up dressing for the "sexy" and instead dress to be the holy, beautiful, feminine women that God made us to be.

We need to set this example and standard for our daughters, our sisters, and the other women in the world. They too need to see that it's possible to be attractive and modest at the same time. I know some people believe the lie that's it's impossible to look attractive and be modest. If you think this, just go outside for a moment and look at everything God has made. He invented beauty—look at the flowers, the grass, the hills, the mountains, and the sky. Everything that God has made is beautiful, and that includes you and me.

If you're a mom raising a daughter in this culture, you have your work cut out for you. However, the grace of God is with you. God gave you that beautiful daughter or granddaughter for you to protect. Right now, you don't need to be her best friend. Be her mom. Set standards. Enforce those standards. Go out of your way to help her find the cutest clothes and the trendiest colors, fabrics, and accessories, and show her that being a modest Jesus-loving girl is absolutely the best life possible.

Does all of this mean that any woman or girl who dresses in a seductive fashion is not a born-again Christian? That decision is not for you or me to make. Let's leave that decision to the only Righteous Judge— Jesus Christ. He alone knows, and all of His judgments are perfectly just. The truth is we are all at different levels of maturity in our Christian lives, and some of us have had better role models in our mothers, aunts, and Sunday school teachers than others. That's why I want to be extra gentle here. It's also quite possible to wear a turtleneck every single day and a skirt down to your ankles and be riddled with lust and looking for men's attention. We can trust God to make righteous and fair judgments in all these matters.

THE CHOICE: HOURGLASS OR MAGNIFYING GLASS

We don't need to be the kind of believers who point the finger. We do what's right in our lives according to our convictions. We model what's right. We speak the Word of God as the Holy Spirit opens the door, and we allow Him to do the work and bring the results.

There are many hurting women and girls looking for love in all the wrong places. Some of them have been abused, ignored, and abandoned. Some of them know better and others don't. Jesus loves every one of us just as we are, and He invites us to have a personal relationship with Him. His deepest desire is that we are all magnifying glasses of His love, grace, and beauty. We can be so attractive that other women and girls want the confidence, assurance, and beauty that we have in Jesus Christ.

Are you ready today to give up the hourglass for the magnifying glass?

Chapter 4

Whose Mirror Are You Looking Into?

We cannot entertain the noise in our heads and give place to God's truth about who we are at the same time. After all, the noise in our head, (our silent critic) feeds our fears and insecurities, and keeps us bound by lies and deceptions of this world and its standard of beauty.

We have the choice each day to decide whose mirror we will look into and whose mirror we will believe. We can dare to believe the Mirror of God's Word through faith, or we can allow the mirror of the world to define our value and beauty. Sometimes we give lip service to God's truth while living another reality in our day-to-day existence.

Here's what I mean. We intellectually and perhaps even verbally say with ease and a smile on our faces that we're beautiful and made in the image of God. Then we scoff as we pass a mirror and see our reflection from an angle that we don't think is our "best side." We cry as we step on the scale, or we hide as we eat a cookie. Secretly, in the quiet corners of our minds, we compare ourselves with the other women/ girls in the room. *Am I the heaviest? Am I the thinnest? Am I the best/worst dressed? Is my nose the biggest one in this room?* The list goes on, and you can fill in your particular struggle here.

In other words, our intellectual understanding that we are beautiful and made in the image of God is not necessarily the truth that grounds us. So, I ask you, whose mirror are you looking into daily?

For many years, and even now on occasion, I still live in that place. I somehow simultaneously know my value and significance comes from God alone, and yet I battle with feeling fat, unworthy, and looking old. I know that I'm made in His image and that He cares for me, and yet I still want to gaze into the mirror of this world and achieve some standard that I feel will make me feel satisfied and commended.

Let Go of Double-Mindedness

It's double-minded, I know. It's insane really. It's like trying to live according to God's Word and somehow being okay with the world as well. God's Word

WHOSE MIRROR ARE YOU LOOKING INTO?

says clearly that friendship with the world is the equivalent of being His enemy. We cannot love God and be a friend of the world too—yet we try. We try on so many levels in this life, but those other levels are subjects for other books. For now, we'll stick with laying down the mirror of this world and its standard and beauty and picking up the Mirror of God's Word and talk about what we really look like according to His perspective.

Let me share a story with you to clarify what I am speaking about:

For years, I longed to be thin. I wanted to fit in with the thin girls at school and my thin female family members. I detested being the chubby girl. I knew that God loved and valued me, yet I also longed to be accepted by thin family members and girls at school. I understood intellectually that I was fearfully and wonderfully made, but secretly I hated my thighs and the size of clothing I wore. I wasted many days, nights, and weekends hating my body and developing unsuccessful diet plans that included eating less than five hundred calories a day. All the while, life was happening all around me and I was missing out.

For a few years, some of my extended female family members weighed in every Sunday after dinner. I mean they literally weighed in on the scale. It was like torture to me. They took turns one after another and they weighed in somewhere between one hundred five and one hundred twenty pounds. I was

73

well over one hundred forty pounds at five feet three inches tall, and whenever it was my turn to get on the scale, I cringed inside. On more than one occasion, I prayed to pass out in order to escape this personal torture after Sunday dinner. In case you're wondering, that seriously flawed prayer was never answered.

I could have elected to pass the weigh-in after Sunday dinner. I mean honestly, who weighs in *after dinner*. No one made me participate. It was a Sunday after-dinner ritual, and I followed what everyone else did. I didn't have enough courage to opt out. At any stage of life, it can be challenging to go against the grain. I know most families and friends don't literally weigh in after Sunday dinner, but we are all asked in some way to participate in the world's system. When our friends talk about how fat they feel or how bad their hair looks, we have the choice to participate and measure ourselves by those same standards, or we can choose to draw the line and say, "I will not accept those worldly definitions as my truth."

We talked about it earlier, but it bears repeating that the world is not going to stop with its vicious attacks on what we need to look like in order to be beautiful and accepted. We have to make the decision to be brave enough to reject the deception and quit measuring ourselves by the mirror of this world.

At this point in our own lives, we need to ask ourselves, *Whose mirror am I looking into?* Are we looking into God's mirror or are we double-mindedly

WHOSE MIRROR ARE YOU LOOKING INTO?

looking into His Mirror while keeping an eye on the World's Mirror?

How much attention to our physical bodies and appearance is too much?

Sometimes it's hard to tell how much attention to our physical bodies and appearance is too much. What is the difference between caring for our bodies as the Temple of the Holy Spirit and putting too much of a priority on our body size and appearance?

I'd like to list a formula that will show clearly what is enough and what is too much. There is, however, no exact measurement in this regard. However, there are some ways to tell whether you are using God's Word as your Mirror or gazing intently into the world's mirror.

When it comes to your physical appearance, where do you find your thoughts, self-talk, and attention tending to gravitate? Are you mostly saying or thinking to yourself:

I'm too fat!

I look old!

My skin is too pale.

My nose is too big.

I'm not as attractive as other women and girls are.

My thighs are huge.

75

I'm too dark.

I have "chicken legs."

If only I could look like her.

I have too many zits.

If you find yourself moving mostly toward negative, critical thoughts about your physical appearance, then you are most definitely looking into the world's mirror to define your beauty and subsequent worth.

When it comes to exercise, which is good for our health when approached the right way and with a physician's approval, do you find yourself thinking:

I need to work out harder/longer than I did yesterday.

I should skip church or an outing with a friend in order to work out.

I will feel very guilty if I can't work out today, even if it's for a good reason.

If you can't work out on a particular day do you find yourself worried that you'll gain weight or fall behind in some way?

Are you afraid if you don't push yourself beyond your limits, then the workout just doesn't count?

Do you feel like you're worth more on days when you can work out than on days when you don't?

Do you avoid any type of exercise because you fear what others will think of you, or you're worried you won't be able to keep up?

I think you get the idea here. As long as a physician or medical professional says that you can work out, then it's good for your health to do so. It's wise to take care of your body. That's a part of being a good steward. When the workout owns you—when you are obsessed with working out or feel like your worth is tied to exercise—then the workout has become an idol. Nothing should take precedence over God in your life. If you're depending on your workout for your beauty, value, or affirmation, then it's out of balance in your life.

Asking yourself these types of questions will help you pinpoint whether you are looking in the world's mirror or God's Mirror. In the Mirror of God's Word, even when something is off kilter or needs improvement in our lives, we feel the gentle, loving nudge and supernatural assistance of the Holy Spirit. Assistance from the Holy Spirit always includes His grace and supernatural power to give us the desire and strength we need in order to change. When we belong to Christ, we are never alone.

Negative, critical condemning thoughts are always from the enemy, the world's system, or our own flesh. God *never* puts us down. He gave us Jesus to lift us up and gives us everything we need for life and godliness.

John 10:10 (NLT)

The thief's purpose is to steal and kill and destroy.

My purpose is to give them a rich and satisfying life.

When it comes to your physical appearance or exercise, do you mostly feel condemned, worried, and concerned with making sure you "measure up?" If you're answer is yes, or mostly yes, or even sometimes yes, then there is some room for growth and change. This life, however, is not a journey to obtain more information. It's not enough to know whether you mostly look into the world's mirror or not. This journey is about trusting and relying on God to give us the strength and power we need to let go of the old (this includes living by the mirror of the world's standards) and embrace new life in Christ (which includes the Mirror of God's Word, which says you are made in His image, finely crafted and beautiful).

One of the things we must understand is that God sent Jesus to give us true and abundant life. His intent was never for His daughters or sons to live life according to the mirror of the world. If after asking yourself that list of questions you found that you are relying on the world's standards to define you, know that Jesus is more than willing to help you change that. Again, many of us want a formula or quick fix chart

WHOSE MIRROR ARE YOU LOOKING INTO?

for change. It doesn't work that way, but God does promise that when we ask for help, He will answer.

The struggle with relying on the world's mirror is intense for most women and girls. If you know that you need to change mirrors but don't know if you have the strength to do so on your own, ask God to change your heart this moment. Here are some good activities to start with:

> Pray and ask God to create in you an intense desire for His Word.
>
> Read God's Word regularly.
>
> Memorize Scripture.
>
> Print Scripture on cards, and carry them around and read them when you're tempted to listen to the world's lies.
>
> Surround yourself with godly friends who will love, honor, and encourage you.

Chapter 5

The Shortsighted Mirror

It was a morning much like any other morning, except that I decided to tweeze my eyebrows. I don't know what your mornings are typically like, but usually I just don't have time in the morning for brow tweezing. For whatever reason, on this particular morning I decided to go ahead and take the extra time to pluck my eyebrows.

In order to make the task easier, I decided to use my lighted magnification mirror—the kind of mirror that makes you look at least ten times larger than you are in real life. I set up the mirror and plugged it in. I reached into my makeup bag and grabbed the tweezers in preparation to pluck away. However, what I saw in this magnification mirror frightened me. It didn't look like a small tweezing job. It looked scary. In the magnifying mirror, it looked like I had gone a year without tweezing my brows.

That's what it's like when we magnify things. They become much larger than they are in real life. In my tweezing dilemma, I was able to forge ahead and complete the job. I was able to go to work and be productive because I understood that even though the eyebrow image was scary, I was looking into a magnifying mirror. What I saw appeared much larger than what it was in real life. Even regular mirrors are shortsighted, as they don't show the whole picture.

My prayer is that as we journey through this book, we'll see that many of our dilemmas, fears, and perceived flaws in appearance are similar to my eyebrow tweezing experience in that —we're not really seeing the overall picture. We're seeing just one part of the whole picture, and we're magnifying a minute portion as if it's the whole thing. At best, it's shortsighted; at worst, it can keep us from seeing the totality of who we really are in Christ, and that is catastrophic.

Reality Check in the Mirror of God's Word

This is where doing our reality check in the Mirror of God's Word makes all the difference. We can either choose to magnify the things we've determined are flaws, or we can decide to believe God's Word about our value, worth, and beauty. The mirror we use to

THE SHORTSIGHTED MIRROR

ensure that our hair is in place is shortsighted. It's just a glimpse of our outward reflection. The mirror can't reflect your inner self or measure your true value. We are more than our reflection in the mirror.

While the mirror is limited to the outward reflection, God lives beyond these limitations. He sees both our outer reflection and our inner selves. He cares about both. He created and designed our outer appearance, and He's committed Himself through His Son Jesus Christ to form in our inner nature the character of Christ as we choose to yield and obey.

While we don't know what Jesus looked like while He walked on earth in the form of a man, we do know from Scripture that He wasn't outwardly attractive by worldly standards.

Isaiah 53:1-3 (KJV)

Who hath believed our report? And to whom is the arm of the Lord revealed? For he shall grow up before him as a tender plant, and as a root out of a dry ground: he hath no form nor comeliness; and when we shall see him, there is no beauty that we should desire him. He is despised and rejected of men; a man of sorrows, and acquainted with grief: and we hid as it were our faces from him; he was despised, and we esteemed him not.

This scripture makes it clear to me, that if measuring up to a worldly scale in our physical form was important to God, then Jesus would have been "off the charts" in terms of physical attractiveness. So what does it mean that he didn't rate in terms of His physical appearance? At the very least, it means that the world's perception of physical attractiveness is not of primary concern to God. Does it mean God doesn't care at all about our physical appearance? I don't think so. Everything God creates is beautiful and has value, however, the world does not measure things or people the same way God does. We are made in His image, and consequently this makes every one of us beautiful and of great value. This world, the devil, and our own flesh has absolutely no right to deem any person or physical feature as *ugly,* or less than attractive or desirable.

What may not have occurred to us is that every time we say something negative about ourselves, we are really saying that God made a mistake in our design. Of course, we know this really isn't the case; it's just that we've been so entrenched in this world's system and scale that we've accepted it as truth without question. By current worldly standards, we believe that thinner is better, oval face shapes are the most desirable, tall is preferable to short, and long, lean legs are best, but who made these decisions anyway?

This is why renewing our minds in God's Word is so critical to our daily existence. It's imperative that we exchange the system of this world for God's absolute truth. This includes our physical appearance, value, and worth. We are finely crafted by God Himself. This makes us all beautiful. Certainly, we

THE SHORTSIGHTED MIRROR

do our part to steward the gift of life that He gives to us. This includes proper hygiene, healthy eating, and adequate exercise. This does not mean a lifetime of stringent dieting, self-loathing, and always wishing for the looks and/or body type that we don't have.

At this point, I'd like to introduce you to G. Joyce Stark. She fulfills many roles in this life. One of them includes heading a ministry in her community called Raise the Praise. I met Joyce at a women's event where I had the pleasure of hearing her speak. I knew when I heard her speak that I needed to get to know her better. Clearly, Joyce has a heart for God and a heart for His people.

Let's listen as G. Joyce Stark shares her heart with us:

> Hey, beautiful! Yes, you who are reading this, I want you to know you are *so* beautiful. I know you're saying, "How can you say I'm beautiful; you don't know me, you've never met me, nor can you see me, so how do you know I'm beautiful?" Oh, that's an easy question to answer. God has never, and He will never, make junk. He says, "You are fearfully and wonderfully made" (Psalm 139:14). He created you in His image. We are not what we look like outwardly; what is inside defines us. We are beautiful spiritual beings living inside a decaying body of flesh. What we appear

85

to be outwardly cannot compare to, nor does it even resemble, our true beauty and who we shall be. Oh, the beauty of who we really are is incredible. Our eyes have not seen, nor have our ears heard, nor has it entered into our hearts what God has planned for us, and that includes our eternal beauty.

I know in today's culture that Proverbs 31:30 isn't a very popular saying.

Proverbs 31:30 (ESV)

Charm is deceitful, and beauty is vain, but a woman who fears the LORD is to be praised.

Nonetheless, it is true. Sadly, we have allowed a culture of marketing vultures to determine our value, our worth, and how we should dress, look, and behave. We have submitted to a god—the beauty industry— and it will ultimately destroy us and cause us never to realize that our true beauty is not determined by our outward appearance. Sadly, many young girls have already been destroyed by this vicious industry.

Let me give you an example. Let's say, for instance, I have child who has never been exposed to this culture's vicious demands and its

THE SHORTSIGHTED MIRROR

deceptive marketing strategies. Let's say my child has been born with an outward physical disability or a facial deformity, but that disability has never been made an issue or exploited. From day one, I have loved and encouraged my child. As my child grows, she views herself by what I have told her repeatedly: "You are so precious. You are so beautiful to me, and you're everything I've hoped for; you're everything I need. You are so beautiful to me." When my child goes to the mirror, she sees herself through my love and realizes the value of whom she truly is—a value that has never been determined by the vain beauty exploited by a corrupt culture. Her view of herself hasn't been distorted by a culture that is soaked in greed, tarnished by sin, and twisted by deception. She views herself through the eyes of love.

God views *you* through the eyes of His love, and he created you out of His love. Don't allow yourself to be destroyed by unattainable goals from an industry and a culture that are vile and corrupt. These goals can never satisfy. Go look in the mirror and repeat these words:

87

"I am fearfully and wonderfully made."
You *are*, you know.

Prayer

Precious Father, Your Word says that charm is deceitful and beauty is vain, but that a woman who fears the Lord is to be praised. Father, I ask you today in Jesus' Name to shape me into a woman who fears you more than anyone or anything else in this world.

In Jesus' Name,

Amen

Reflection Time

When you read the first line in this devotional that said "Hey, beautiful," how did you feel? Did you wince? Did you hesitate?

Are you willing to see yourself as the beautiful woman/girl whom God made you to be?

Have you or are you currently allowing the media or various marketing campaigns to define your value?

Meditate on this Scripture:

Proverbs 31:30

Charm is deceitful, and beauty is vain, but a woman who fears the LORD is to be praised.

Read it aloud. Write it down. Post it on Facebook. Go ahead and put it on Twitter. Do whatever you can to saturate yourself with these words. May we all understand together as sisters in Christ that a woman who fears the Lord is to be praised! This is where we need to focus our time, hearts, and thoughts.

In other words, we need to magnify the Word of God in our lives. We need to take a moment to realize that even the most powerful beautifying routine pales in comparison to a woman who truly fears the Lord. It's not our beauty or charm for which we should be praised, but our holy fear of the Lord. We appreciate praise and compliments from others on our new outfits and haircuts, and not all of that is bad. It just needs to be in proper perspective. If we live solely or even mostly for the affirmation of others, we miss at least part of the purpose and plan God has for our lives.

Living out God's Purpose

Living out God's purpose and plan for us makes our lives fulfilling and beautiful. There's nothing like walking out the plan designed for us by our Creator. When we walk in obedience to God's word and recognize our true beauty and value in Him, our priorities change. I'd like you to meet best-selling author and speaker Karol Ladd. She brings an important perspective to us in terms of how we reflect His character in our being. Reflecting His nature in our lives brings beauty to us and to those around us.

Here is what Karol Ladd has to say:

> How wonderful to know we were designed by God. The Bible tells us He created us in His likeness.

Colossians 1:16 (NIV)

For in him all things were created.

> We reflect His character in our being. Our ability to create, to connect, to love, to show patience, to give kindness, to offer forgiveness, all reflect His nature. Knowing God created us in His likeness gives us a sense of worth and purpose. God placed His nature in you and in me. He created us, and He does not make mistakes. Sadly, there are times when we hear a voice whisper in our ear, "You are worthless. There is no purpose for your life." These are lies from the enemy. You are a creation of God almighty. He knew exactly what He was doing when He created you. Listen to His voice saying, "My beloved daughter, I knew you in your mother's womb. You didn't just happen. I formed you, I created you, and I have a purpose for your life."

THE SHORTSIGHTED MIRROR

Never forget that you were created by Him. He knows your name. He knows your challenges. He understands your pain. He loves you as His precious creation. Take time each day to thank the Lord for creating you. I'm not suggesting to say it in a prideful way, such as, "Well, isn't the world lucky to have me." Rather, I'm encouraging you to pray in a humble way, "Thank you, Lord, that you created me. All that I am comes from you. Thank you that you have a purpose for me, and you have equipped me exactly for that purpose." Do you see how that prayer takes away pride, yet builds confidence in God?

Satan would love for you to forget each day that you are God's creation formed by His loving hands. Let us live each day with God-confidence, knowing we are formed by His design, and that He has a plan and a purpose for every single one of us.

"Choose to accept and become the person God has made you to be."

– John Mason

Prayer

Dear Father,

I pray for the grace and willingness to accept and become the person you made me to be.

In Jesus' Name,

Amen

Reflection Time

What specific practical things can I do or think today to demonstrate that I am willing to accept and become the person God made me to be?

Take a few moments to reflect on how wonderful it is to be designed by God.

Make the choice today to walk in the knowledge (silence that inner critic) that you are formed by His design and that He has a unique plan and purpose for your life.

As we make the choice today to walk in the knowledge of God's design and purpose for our lives, we need also to understand that words are packed with power. We hear words every day that tell us who or what we should be, and what we could do differently or better next time. The words we hear can make us feel happy or sad, or perhaps even inadequate.

THE SHORTSIGHTED MIRROR

Jennifer Brindley-Webster will join our conversation at this point. She's an expert in nutrition and fitness, and she's the television host of the *Rise Up* workout show on the NRB network and other television stations.

Let's listen as Jennifer Brindley-Webster shares her heart with us:

> It's important that we allow God's Word to define us rather than the words of other people. With that in mind, I would like to share a story of a major change from my personal life. During this time, it was as if my identity hinged on the opinions of others. If I received a compliment, I felt happy, but if I was criticized, I collapsed into depression. The problem was that people's opinions change constantly, and since my identity was connected to what others thought, I found myself going up and down emotionally.
>
> Finally, I discovered that God's Word *always* has something good to say about me and that I can make the decision to believe God's Word or believe the words of others. What I love about God's Word is that it is unchanging, so if your identity is anchored in the Word of God, you will be consistent and

unchanging. One man said, "We can be so filled with God's Word and God's Spirit that when the enemy launches an attack against us, he has so much of the Word of God and the Spirit of God to get through that by the time he gets to us, he is already defeated. However, if your self-worth, value, or image is based on what people say, you have set yourself up for defeat."

1 Peter 1:24-25 (KJV)

For all flesh is as grass, and all the glory of man as the flower of grass. The grass withereth, and the flower thereof falleth away: But the word of the Lord endureth forever. And this is the word which by the gospel is preached unto you.

Stop allowing other people to define you. When you allow God's Word to define you, people will begin to discover you.

Dear Father,

I come to you today in Jesus' name and ask for the strength and power to unhook my identity from the comments of others, and instead to fully base my iden-

THE SHORTSIGHTED MIRROR

tity on who you made me to be in Christ. Father, your Word endures forever, and I pray for my identity to be totally based on your unchanging Word.

In Jesus' Name,

Amen

Reflection Time

Have you ever based your opinion of yourself on the comments of others?

If you have done this, has it seemed like an unpleasant roller coaster ride?

Do you find yourself seeking compliments or the approval of others?

Have you ever really tried to detach yourself from the system of this world (basing your identity on what others say) to basing your identity on what God's Word says?

Are you ready to try that today? I pray you are with all my heart.

Write down some of the things people have said about you that you have accepted as the truth about your value. Next to that, write God's truth about your beauty and value

Today's scripture is 1 Peter 1:24-25, which says that the Word of the Lord stands forever.

95

Yep, that's right; what God says about you, that you are made in His image and finely crafted, is *true forever*. Print and carry this scripture around with you in a place where you will see it often. If someone makes an unkind comment about you or your appearance, make it a point to remind yourself of God's unchanging truth about whom you are

As we remind ourselves of God's unchanging truth, we are encouraging ourselves in the Lord and declaring that the world's mirror is, at best, shortsighted. We cannot afford to allow the mirror to define our beauty, value, or worth. So many opinions and so many voices will try to define us or tell us that we are pretty or that we are not, but God has already spoken about our worth and our true beauty. We need to give Him our attention and listen to His voice.

With that in mind, Donna Johnson will share her heart as we share and study together on this journey of finding our identity and value in Jesus Christ. Donna Johnson is a wife, mom, writer, blogger, medical transcriptionist, and my little sister.

Let's listen as Donna Johnson shares her heart with us:

True North

So many voices and so many opinions,
each telling me who I am, who I should
aspire to be, and each one reminding me,
most definitely, who I am not. Sometimes

THE SHORTSIGHTED MIRROR

the voices are so loud, and I feel so small. There is very real pressure to be what the world considers pleasing and acceptable. The media tells me to be the right size, to have the right clothes, to hide the wrinkles, cover the gray, get rid of the zit, to plump it up and suck it in—I have to keep trying harder because at the most basic level, I'm just not good enough. Then I hear Him—I hear the Truth.

A choice comes with each new day. Whose voice will I listen to and follow today? Who and what will I allow to define me? I choose my Creator, the One who knit me together and is interested in the details of my life, the One who hems me in with His great care. He is my Creator and the Maker of all my moments.

Father, you alone have the right to define me. What a blessing beyond measure it is to be fully known and fully loved unconditionally and completely. This beautiful truth is ours for the taking with no strings and no empty promises. Nothing can change that simple, powerful, and perfect Truth.

Some days are so hard and so distracting, and I lose my way. I fall into old habits and insecurities, but then I hear His Voice reminding me that He is ever near. I hear the Truth. With each new day comes a new choice, and sometimes I must make that choice moment by moment and cling to the Truth when everything around me is pulling me to go a different way.

So today, I am being bold and charting a course for True North. Today I am daring to renew my mind. Today I celebrate my weakness because You are my strength. Today I celebrate and confess my great need for you and my inability to do anything of lasting significance apart from you. Father, today and always, I am wholly yours.

Psalm 139:13-16 (MSG)

Oh yes, you shaped me first inside, then out; you formed me in my mother's womb. I thank you, High God—you're breathtaking! Body and soul, I am marvelously made! I worship in adoration—what a creation! You know me inside and out, you know every bone in my body; You know exactly how I was made, bit by bit, how I was sculpted from nothing into something. Like an open book, you watched me grow from conception to birth; all the stages of my life were spread out before you,

THE SHORTSIGHTED MIRROR

The days of my life all prepared before I'd even lived one day.

Prayer

Dear Father,

In Jesus' Name, guide me today to your Truth—your powerful, perfect Truth. I pray that today your voice will be louder than any other sound I might hear. I choose, Father, to obey you and your Word today. Jesus, I will follow you today. Please open the doors you have charted out for me today and close the doors that need to be closed.

In Jesus' Name,

Amen

Reflection Time

List some of the opinions other have expressed to you about who you are.

Now list what God says to you about your life, your value, and your worth.

Are you willing to accept God's Truth about your beauty, value, and worth above what others have said to you?

Are you willing to forgive those who may have spoken negative words (knowingly or not) about your beauty, your value, and your life?

Do you know that forgiveness of those who have wronged you will release you from a prison of torment?

If you need help in extending forgiveness to others, God will help you. Just ask Him. He is the friend that sticks closer than a brother. He is our help, refuge, and strength in our time of trouble.

Let your mind reflect for just a few moments on God's love toward you, which is so complete and so unconditional. The more you reflect on His love, the more beauty you will see in your life.

God Wants to Do Miracles Inside of Us

The mirror is so shortsighted, and God knows no limitations. He knew what He was doing when He created you and me. He wants to impart to us the character of His dear Son Jesus Christ. While the world is controlled by outward appearances, God wants to do miracles within us. He wants to give us patience, love, kindness, gentleness, and mercy to bring out what's truly beautiful in our lives and communities. Of course, we won't stop with good grooming routines, but we won't neglect looking to Him and depending on Him to renew our inner selves with His goodness.

Galatians 5:22-23 (MSG)

But what happens when we live God's way? He brings gifts into our lives, much

THE SHORTSIGHTED MIRROR

the same way that fruit appears in an orchard—things like affection for others, exuberance about life, serenity. We develop a willingness to stick with things, a sense of compassion in the heart, and a conviction that a basic holiness permeates things and people. We find ourselves involved in loyal commitments, not needing to force our way in life, able to marshal and direct our energies wisely.

None of the above attributes can be seen in the world's mirror, but these are the attributes that give our lives substance and meaning. These attributes are far more important than what we see in the mirror or read on the scale. In God's economy, these attributes are truly beautiful, and they are available to all believers so that we can make Christ known throughout the world.

Go ahead and tell the mirror that it's flawed and distorted. Thank God that He sees everything as it really is, and He does all things well.

James 1:18 (NLT)

He chose to give birth to us by giving us his true word. And we, out of all creation, became his prized possession.

Did you know out of all creation that we are God's prized possession? We are His favorite, so don't let any shortsighted mirror tell you anything differently.

Chapter 6

Shattering the Mirror of the World

Can you hear the sound of the world's mirror shattering in response to the Truth of God's Word? Every time we expose a lie of the world and replace it with God's truth, the lie is shattered, the deception is dispelled, and the Light of the World (Jesus) illuminates and fills our world with true and lasting beauty. God's Word is powerful and has the ability to shatter every lie you have ever believed about your beauty, value or anything else in your life.

Are you at a place right now where you need to ask yourself honestly if you are willing to lay down the lies you've believed about yourself? As you ask the Holy Spirit to show you what you need to lay down, you might be surprised. You may have been carrying a pack of lies for so long that you no longer see the deception. It may be like looking into a mirror that has those annoying streaks from using window cleaner and paper towels. You know those streaks on the mirror that you just can't get rid of? You spray the cleaner and wipe away with the paper towel, but those annoying streaks are still there (if you've found a way around this problem – please let me know, I am eager to learn). The end result is that the mirror still shows us our reflection, but it's distorted. That's what it's like when we believe what the world says about beauty.

Perhaps you've lived with the distorted reality that only thin women are beautiful, or that looking like a twenty-something is the ultimate objective for every woman. It may be that you're always on a diet. You may weigh, measure, and count every piece of food you eat. You may feel that the more closely you follow your diet, the more beautiful and valuable you are. You may work out regularly or stringently to the point of exhaustion. All of these things can be distortions. None of these routines are mentioned in the Bible.

Now, I am not telling you not to eat healthy food. I eat healthy foods regularly and eat treats moderately. I am not saying don't work out (I do). I certainly would not tell you not to wear fashionable clothes, as I also like pretty clothes and good bargains. What I am saying is that these things do not solely define our

SHATTERING THE MIRROR OF THE WORLD

beauty and value. These things are not the ultimate goal of our lives, nor should they absorb all of our time, thoughts, and energy. These things do not make us more "I've got it all together" Jesus-loving Christian girls. These things are actually much like brushing and flossing our teeth. We do them because they are good for us, but we do not make them *idols* in our lives or rely on them for our identity.

We are made in His image. We are fearfully and wonderfully made. We are made to be in a relationship with God through His Son Jesus Christ. We are made to be in fellowship with our sisters and brothers in Christ. We are made to be in relationships with Him and others. We are made to enjoy relationships—giving and receiving comfort. We are made to celebrate, connect, and lead purpose-filled lives. These things are grossly hindered when our value is tied to being thin or to a number on the scale. We are missing the wonderful plan God has for us if we are focused on striving for a certain physical appearance, and feeling down and out because we've judged who we are by the world's standards. If we feel we've come up lacking in this regard, and this has occupied major time in our head, heart, wallet, or relationships then we are missing the wonderful plan God has for our lives, families, and friendships.

Once we shatter the image of ourselves reflected in the mirror of the world, we are released into the Mirror of God's Word. We are then free to obey these scriptures:

105

Mark 12:30-31 (NLT)

And you must love the Lord your God with all your heart, all your soul, all your mind, and all your strength.' The second is equally important: 'Love your neighbor as yourself.' No other commandment is greater than these.

When our value, appearance, or anything else becomes the focus of our lives in an unbalanced way, it becomes an idol. This idol prohibits us from loving and obeying God freely. When we lay down the idol of unbalanced concern over our appearance, we lose the fear of rejection and the opinions of others. When we're free of these things, we can love and obey God more freely.

Love Our Neighbor as We Love Ourselves

Another thing that happens when we become too focused on our physical appearance is that we limit the opportunity to develop good, honest relationships with others. Truly, if we're majorly tied up with excessive dieting, and our emotional well-being is connected to how much we weigh, it's hard to really love our neighbors because we don't love ourselves. It's difficult to connect and laugh with others when our major concerns are about the size of our thighs. Can you imagine even for a brief moment what it would have been like for the woman who needed to be

SHATTERING THE MIRROR OF THE WORLD

healed of the issue of blood if Jesus had been overly concerned with his physical appearance that day? It seems outrageous to think that even for a moment. Does it seem outrageous that we may be missing similar opportunities because we're at home lamenting that we've gained five pounds instead of getting out there meeting people, serving others, sharing Jesus, and living life to its fullest?

Take just a few moments here and really think about it. Are there things you will not do until you lose some weight? Are there opportunities that you shrink back from because you feel that you look inadequate in some way? Are there hurting people around you who you could be unintentionally overlooking because you're trying so hard to look picture-perfect? Could it be that you are partially short-circuiting God's plan for your life because you've allowed the mirror or someone else's opinion to tell you that you're inadequate—that you can't do something, that you shouldn't, or that you'll fail if you do?

I'm inviting Shana Shutte to join us now. She's a speaker, an author, and a God-fearing woman who knows that with God, all things are possible.

Here is what Shanna Shutte has to say:

> Throughout our lives, we encounter many people who tell us what we cannot accomplish.

> "You can't be a chemist. You're not analytical enough."
>
> "You can't be a professional singer. You're not attractive enough."
>
> "There is no way you'll make it as a teacher. You're not patient enough."
>
> "You must be kidding! You want to be a pastor's wife? You won't be a good role model."
>
> As we get older, sometimes we are still waiting for someone else to tell us that it's okay to "cross the street" to our God-given destiny.
>
> But remember this: Because God made you, He perfectly equipped you for your God-given mission. Therefore, the only leader you need to seek for approval is God. There will be times when others won't see what He sees in you. Your friends may tell you that it can't be done. But if He has placed a dream in you, there is nothing that can stop you from achieving it for Him.

It's important to really consider what Shanna is saying. First, there will always be people who are filled with ideas about what we can and cannot do. That won't ever change. What we can change is our per-

SHATTERING THE MIRROR OF THE WORLD

spective by shattering the world's mirror and embracing God's Mirror as our absolute truth.

It's a big decision to lay down the mirror of the world, but it's the best commitment you'll ever make. Rejecting the world's standard and embracing the Mirror of God's Word will change you and everyone around you. That prodigal child can't help but be positively influenced when she sees you recognize your value and worth in Jesus Christ. The hard-to-please boss will see you as a brand new employee as you put on a smile and embrace a can-do attitude because you are no longer dependent on him or her for affirmation—you are sure of who you are in Christ.

The more like Jesus we become, the more we will affect those around us for His Kingdom. We can't do that on our own. We can't do that while staring in the mirror and wanting affirmation from this world. We must heed the call to shatter the mirror of the world and hold tight to the Mirror of God's Word and allow His reflection to shine through us like never before.

How much better or lighter would your life be if your days weren't limited by negative self-talk about your weight or looks. What if, as you prepare for your day and glance into the mirror, your overriding question is "Am I prepared to face this day with the strength, dignity, and value of the King's daughter?" instead of "Does this make me look fat?"

We may love the idea of embracing our role on this earth as a daughter of the King. At the same time though, there may be a little fear in the back of our heads asking, "Can I really change?" Is it possible to give up being consumed, or at least overly interested, in appearances? If we take the challenge and shatter the mirror of the world what will happen? We will begin to see the world's standards of beauty as lies that cause us pain. Once we have that revelation, we will no longer strive for the approval of others and try to please God at the same time.

Of course, you and I know it isn't possible to please God and secure the approval of others at the same time, but oh, how we try. We evaluate ourselves in the mirror, by the size of our jeans, the clarity of our complexion, and the list drones on. We must embrace the truth that many of us have spent our lives in front of the carnival's distorting mirror that twists and warps our true reflection. In many cases, that mirror of the world is nothing more than an idol that rules our day.

It may be scary to choose to step down from the mirror of the world. It may even seem impossible, but we can lay it down. As Paul said, we may also say, "I die daily." This battle isn't about a single moment, but a decision lived out in faith every day of our lives.

Some of the Lies We May Believe

Let's identify some of this world's lies about our value and beauty. I'll list a few examples to get

SHATTERING THE MIRROR OF THE WORLD

us started. As you think of lies that you've accepted and believe, list them in your journal so that you can renounce and replace them with the truth.

The thinner I am the more beautiful I am.

I'm too fat.

I'm ugly.

My lips are too big.

My thighs are dimpled and fat.

I can't stand the way I look.

If I were more attractive, people would like me better.

As you list each lie you want to renounce, list the truth right next to it that you will hold on to every day of your life.

For example:

The lie I am renouncing:	*My new Truth:*
The thinner I am the more beautiful I am.	I am beautiful whether I am thin or not.
I'm too fat.	I'm thankful for the body God has given me.

I'm ugly.	I am designed by God.
My lips are too big.	I am God's unique creation.
My thighs are dimpled and fat.	I am thankful to be a woman.

After you have identified the lies and replaced them with the truth, place a line or x through each deception. There is no need to repeat or go back to lies that you've already renounced and replaced with the truth. Focus, speak and magnify the truth.

Every time you focus, speak, and magnify the truth, you are shattering the mirror of the world and the power it has to shape your attitude and thinking. From this day forward, we are sticking with the truth. The mirror of the world has shattered, and you can now see your true reflection.

Get Off the Scale!

You are beautiful. Your beauty, just like your capacity for life, happiness, and success, is immeasurable. Day after day, countless people across the globe get on a scale in search of social acceptance and a validation of their beauty.

Get off the scale! I have yet to see a scale that can tell you how enchanting

SHATTERING THE MIRROR OF THE WORLD

your eyes are. I have yet to see a scale that can show you how wonderful your hair looks when the sun shines its glorious rays on it. I have yet to see a scale that can thank you for your compassion, sense of humor, and contagious smile. Get off the scale because I have yet to see one that can admire you for your perseverance when challenged in life.

It's true; the scale can only give you a numerical reflection of your relationship with gravity. That's it. It cannot measure beauty, talent, purpose, life force, possibility, strength, or love. Don't give the scale more power than it has earned. Take note of the number, then get off the scale and live your life. You are beautiful!

– Steve Maraboli, from his book *Life, the Truth, and Being Free*

Reflection Time

According to a recent poll done by *Glamour* magazine, a whopping 97 percent of women admitted to having at least one "I hate my body" thought each day. Even sadder yet, on average, those women (just about all of us) have thirteen negative thoughts about their bodies per day.

Are you willing, with God's help, to defy the odds and silence the inner critic? Are you willing to reject the lie of this world and let God's Truth about who you really are define your beauty and value?

My prayer is that you answer this question with a resounding **yes**! We can do this. This is our choice. Do we really believe what God says about our beauty, value, and worth? Do we really want to reach out in faith and fulfill God's plan for our lives? I think we do. It's a daily journey, so let's start it now. I think I'm starting to hear the world's mirror shattering. That's definitely music to my ears.

Chapter 7

The Woman in the Mirror

Most of us have spent a lot of time as "the woman in the mirror." We've fixed, straightened, and primped probably more times than we care to count. All of this isn't bad, of course. Who wants to leave the house with uncombed hair or morning breath? The woman in the mirror is worth taking care of and investing time in. We just want to be careful not to go to extremes and tie our value to our weight or our physical appearance.

If the scale shows a five-pound weight gain, or the mirror reveals a less than ideal hair day, and we end up in *meltdown mode*, we can be certain we've gone to the extreme. When these things happen, they are red flags that indicate our lives are out of balance. Rather

115

than let these sorts of things threaten to rule our days, we need to wake up and believe God's truth that we are finely crafted and made in His image. Fashion trends come and go, but God's Word stands forever.

We Are Meant for More

In these *meltdown* moments, we understand that the woman or girl in the mirror was meant for more than perfectly tweezed brows or super white teeth. We are meant to reflect His character. We are designed to reflect His image. The world, the devil, and our own flesh would like to tie our hearts to the woman or girls' reflection in the mirror, but God wants our hearts so that He can conform our inner selves to the image of His Son.

Romans 8:28-30 (NIV)

And we know that in all things God works for the good of those who love him, who have been called according to his purpose. For those God foreknew he also predestined to be *conformed to the image of his Son*, that he might be the firstborn among many brothers and sisters. And those he predestined, he also called; those he called, he also justified; those he justified, he also glorified.

You see right there in the middle of one of the most quoted passages of scripture is something we may accidentally skim over; it's the part where He says He wants to conform us in the image of His Son.

Sometimes, when it comes to the woman in the mirror, we are so busy working to conform her to society's current image ideal that we forget that the ultimate objective for the Jesus-loving girl is to be conformed to the image of God's only Son Jesus Christ.

Romans 10:17 (NLT)

So faith comes from hearing, that is, hearing the Good News about Christ.

James 1:24-25 (MSG)

Don't fool yourself into thinking that you are a listener when you are anything but, letting the Word go in one ear and out the other. Act on what you hear! Those who hear and don't act are like those who glance in the mirror, walk away, and two minutes later have no idea who they are, what they look like. But whoever catches a glimpse of the revealed counsel of God—the free life!—even out of the corner of his eye, and sticks with it, is no distracted scatterbrain but a man or woman of action. That person will find delight and affirmation in the action.

Both of these verses give us insight into how God works in our lives. Our faith comes from hearing the good news of the gospel, and you are blessed when you hear and obey God's Word. The more you hear and obey God's Word, the more like Him you become. You will find that as you hear, obey, and put into practice what He says, you will see His character reflected throughout your life on an ever-increasing basis. Then, you won't have to *try* being patient with others or *work in your own strength* to improve how you treat others. As you hear and obey God's Word, your inner nature will be transformed, and things that were difficult, even impossible, will become possible for you. You will be able to love the unlovable, be patient with those who are hard to get along with, listen to the know-it-all, and show love in any and every situation. This happens as Christ is formed in you. This happens by hearing and obeying God's Word.

The truly beautiful woman's makeover is not an outward thing—it's an inward work completed as Christ resides in our hearts and we put into practice what He tells us in the Bible. As we do this, we are changed and conformed to His image. The woman in the mirror is no longer defined by what she wears, weighs, or how she looks—she lives life as a daughter of the King, and as such, she reflects His good character on a daily basis.

I would like to invite Sheryl Griffin, author, speaker, wife, mom, and friend, to join our conversation. You'll find, as you read what she has to say, that for much of her life she did not feel beautiful. She didn't recognize her value.

As Sheryl Griffin shares her journey, allow her experience to speak to you:

THE WOMAN IN THE MIRROR

As far back as I can recall I never felt beautiful. I struggled with feeling *less than* in many areas of my life. I grew up in a middle-class neighborhood, but as a family, we struggled financially. I was the oldest of six children, and my father was always on unemployment for one reason or another. We frequently lived on public assistance programs and ate free lunches at school. I wore hand-me-downs, and while I dreamed of having beautiful Farrah Fawcett hair, mine was straight, flat, and uninspiring. As a young teen girl I went to sleep at night and prayed that I would look different in the morning, hoping for a miracle to gain the attention that I craved.

I know now that my feelings of insecurity stemmed from issues of guilt, shame, and fear. While these issues plagued me for most of my life, I have learned to trade my feelings of insignificance along with guilt, shame, and fear for confidence, dignity, and self-respect. This process started with my acceptance of who I am in Christ. I also recognized patterns in my life of taking responsibility for other people's choices and feelings. I ignored red flags, and I continually put things under the rug, thinking *If I don't say*

119

anything about this, it will go away. I often felt worthless and unaccepted, and thought my feelings did not matter to anyone else.

I know now that:

I was not an accident...

Psalm 139:13-14 (ESV)

For you formed my inward parts; you knitted me together in my mother's womb. I praise you, for I am fearfully and wonderfully made. Wonderful are your works; my soul knows it very well

God has a plan and a purpose for my life...

Jeremiah 29:11 (ESV)

For I know the plans I have for you, declares the Lord, plans for welfare and not for evil, to give you a future and a hope

I am valued...

Luke 12:7 (ESV)

Why, even the hairs of your head are all numbered. Fear not; you are of more value than many sparrows.

I am rejoiced over...

THE WOMAN IN THE MIRROR

Zephaniah 3:17 (ESV

The Lord your God is in your midst, a mighty one who will save; he will rejoice over you with gladness; he will quiet you by his love; he will exult over you with loud singing.

Romans 8:38-39 (NIV)

For I am convinced that neither death nor life, neither angels nor demons, neither the present nor the future, nor any powers, neither height nor depth, nor anything else in all creation, will be able to separate us from the love of God that is in Christ Jesus our Lord.

The true beauty in all of this is that these scriptures are meant for you as well. You are not an accident, God has a plan and a purpose for your life; you are valued, you are rejoiced over, and nothing can separate you from the love of God.

Prayer

Dear Jesus,

Please open up my heart and life to the truth of your Word. Thank you, Jesus, that I am valued and rejoiced over! Thank you, Jesus, that nothing I've done, suffered, or been through can ever separate me from your love. Open my eyes to your perspective and your beautiful plan for my life today.

In Jesus' Name,

Amen

Reflection Time

Have you struggled with insecurity, fear, guilt, or shame? Are you currently struggling with any of these?

Are you willing to stop for a moment today and just soak up the love that God has for you in His Son Jesus Christ?

Would you take a moment right now to allow yourself to hear Him rejoice over you with singing?

There are no *accidents* with God.

You have just read that your life is not an accident. Do you believe that? Your life is not an accident, but a part of God's plan, and this means that you are significantly valued. How does this make you feel?

Look into His Mirror right now. See the beauty and the plan that He has for you. It's a good plan. It's better than you've ever imagined.

Isn't it comforting to know that our lives are not an accident? Just understanding that the Creator of the universe rejoices over me gives me encouragement for today and tomorrow. We struggle for many reasons, but one of them is simply that we were born into a culture entrenched in magnifying the importance of our outward appearance.

A lot of us don't know anything else. We've never really imagined a world without all of our conveniences. Many of us have never known a life minus a curling or flat iron. That's why I asked Shanda Tripp, wife, mom, pastor, television host, and missionary kid to hang out with us for a while. She had the privilege of being on the mission field as a child and seeing first-hand what a truly beautiful person really looks like.

Let's listen as Shanda Tripp shares her heart with us:

I believe a truly beautiful person is the one looking at Jesus.

Psalms 139:14 (NKJV)

"I will praise You, for I am fearfully and wonderfully made; Marvelous are Your works, And that my soul knows very well."

In this modern world, it has become normal to go to the doctor and have something nipped, tucked, lifted, or surgically removed, all in the name of beauty. People are constantly in a competition with societal illusions of what "true beauty" entails.

I had the privilege of spending my childhood on the foreign mission field. Being the daughter of missionaries, I have had the privilege to visit many remote places—villages so remote there was no electricity, no running water, or modern conveniences that we in America take so for granted.

I believe I have witnessed true beauty. It is a lady stepping out of a mud hut wearing clothes she has washed by hand—clean as a spring morning. Her hair is beautifully crafted in her native style, and her eyes are more beautiful than a doctor could ever enhance. She has a smile that lights the day. She has a tattered family Bible under her arm, and she's ready to walk to church. She will worship her Creator, the One who supplies all her needs. She has found her self-worth by looking to Jesus. This lady has learned the secret to true beauty, and she knows that it only comes from Him. The world does not define her worth or beauty. She only looks to Jesus!

Search your heart today. Have you found your true beauty in Him? It is available as you acknowledge and

THE WOMAN IN THE MIRROR

praise your Creator and Savior, Jesus Christ.

Prayer

Dear Father,

I come to you hungering and thirsting for your righteousness today. I come to you, Jesus, and ask you to fill my life with your Light and the Beauty of your Word. Father, let me see who I am in your Son, Jesus Christ. May the truth of who I am in Christ speak more loudly to me than the voice of the world. I love you, Jesus, and I pray that your plan for my life will be fulfilled.

In Jesus' Name,

Amen

Reflection Time

Have I found my true beauty in Jesus Christ?

In what ways am I defining my beauty or value according to the world's standards?

Have I found my identity and self-worth in Jesus? Do I let the lies of this world intimidate me?

How can I replace the lies of this world with God's truth?

Am I looking to Jesus every day of my life? How can I look to Jesus as my refuge, my identity, my helper, and the provider of purpose?

After talking with Shanda, we see that true beauty comes to those who look to Jesus and depend on Him for everything. As we look to Jesus and yield to Him, His character is formed in our lives. As His character is formed inwardly within us, it can't help but overflow to our countenance as well. His character shines in our countenance and in our actions.

In this process of character formation, greed turns to generosity, anger yields to forgiveness; resentment dissipates and is replaced with His love. The woman consumed with the "green-eyed monster" of envy is transformed into a sharing, giving friend. The urge to compete gives way to sharing, and gossip is replaced with edifying conversation. You see, the most beautiful life is found in complete surrender to Christ.

Galatians 5:22-23 (AMP)

But the fruit of the [Holy] Spirit [the work which His presence within accomplishes] is love, joy (gladness), peace, patience (an even temper, forbearance), kindness, goodness (benevolence), faithfulness, Gentleness (meekness, humility), self-control (self-restraint, continence). Against such things there is no law that can bring a charge.

THE WOMAN IN THE MIRROR

The new nature that He gives far exceeds any promise of the world. The value and beauty He gives does not wither over time, and cannot be stolen by experience. The joy found in remaining in Christ is greater than achieving any worldly standard of beauty. It far surpasses the struggle for some standard of perfection that is unrealistic and/or simply out of reach.

The woman or girl we see in the mirror longs for something more. We think we'll be satisfied once we are thin enough, have a tummy tuck, or can fit back into that outfit that's been hanging in our closet for the last two years, but what we really long for is unconditional love, acceptance, and affirmation. That kind of love can't be found by covering up the "flaws" on the woman in the mirror. That kind of love, acceptance, and affirmation comes only from being rooted and grounded in Jesus Christ.

Ephesians 3:16-18 (NLT)

I pray that from his glorious, unlimited resources he will empower you with inner strength through his Spirit. Then Christ will make his home in your hearts as you trust in him. Your roots will grow down into God's love and keep you strong. And may you have the power to understand, as all God's people should, how wide, how long, how high, and how deep his love is.

One of the fears most of us struggle with is that if we yield to Him and reject the world, we'll lose out on the fun in life. Nothing could be further from the truth. When we reject the world, we are free to live in Him. This journey starts by understanding how real and deep His love for you is. It's so much easier to lay down the worldly standards of beauty (the lie) and pick up God's truth about your value and worth when you realize He loves and values you *more* than anybody else ever could.

Bask in His Unconditional Love and Acceptance

If you'll take just a few minutes every day in front of the mirror to remind yourself of His unconditional love for you, and if you'll focus instead on how you are loved, finely crafted, and made in His image, the power of the lies of the world will dissipate from your life. You'll find yourself letting go of those negative, obsessive pulls to weigh yourself every single day, measure your value to the size of your jeans, worry about whether you look good enough, or whether the more attractive woman will get the job, the man, the whatever. You will let go of all that "*wordly stuff*" as you lose yourself in Him. If you'll have just enough faith to believe that God is right and everybody else is wrong, the woman in the mirror will become a brand new person and will relate to herself and others in a brand new way.

What if the woman in the mirror wasn't bound to the opinions of others? What if you didn't have to live

THE WOMAN IN THE MIRROR

or dress to attract or turn the heads of men? What if you didn't have to compete with other women for beauty, style, or attention? What if you could look at the woman in the mirror in a new way?

Could you be convinced that this new way of thinking and relating to others would release you into God's plan for your life? Are you willing to suppose for a moment that perhaps you've been living in a trap, and that you can be set free to be who God really created you to be?

The woman God really created you to be is deep inside of you. The real *you* may have been beaten down by the lies and unrealistic standards of the world. Perhaps the real you has been walked on by people or their insensitive comments. But the real you is still there. God wants to release you so that you can be the real woman He made you to be. Some people wrongly think that to be a Christian woman you have to deny the real you, but that's another lie. There is a real you that God ordained. He wants that real you to come alive in Christ and go forth in what He's called you to do.

Be the Real You

The real you and your God-given call are so important that I invited Nancy Rue, best-selling author, to talk with us for a while about what the Scripture in the Bible really means when it says we are to deny ourselves.

Let's listen as Nancy Rue shares her heart with us:

Which "Self" Do We Deny?

Matthew 16:24 (NRS)

If any want to become my followers, let them deny themselves and take up their cross and follow me.

Many passages of Scripture have been so twisted by interpretation that Jesus Himself probably no longer recognizes them, but few poorly understood verses have done more damage to women than the Scripture quoted above from Matthew.

If I, as a woman, deny myself to follow Christ, does that mean I devote myself entirely to my family, my church obligations, and my blogging for the Lord and not give a thought to me? Am I to give up everything that brings me joy? Is a grande vanilla latte once a week taboo, or a nice coat of nail polish or a lovely decorative pillow for the bed? Does this indicate that applying a little mascara, covering my gray, or feeling pretty cute in my leather boots stands between me and following my Lord?

Make that NO! Jesus is talking about the false self—that persona we start layering on when we hit preschool and discover that some people out there don't have to love us. We have to earn their approval and acceptance, and we aren't altogether sure if who we are is good enough for them. So we figure out what "they" want, and like chameleons, we act accordingly. We pretend, manipulate, fib, and shape ourselves so that we can fit in, and we deny our true selves in the process.

Following Jesus means peeling off the layers of falseness, not the layers of nail color or the other small things we do to enhance our beauty. It means refusing to do what society expects of us, and instead examining whom God made us to be and how we can use that person for Him. Yes, as women, we're natural nurturers, but we're also natural individuals who need as much time for contemplation and the pursuit of our strengths as men do. We must never deny our God-made selves, ladies. So take up the cross, and let Jesus take you on the journey of self-discovery.

Reflection Time

Do you see, perhaps in a new way, how you've denied your true God-given uniqueness to fit in and be accepted? If so, in what ways have you done this?

Are you ready to give up your false persona to embrace the truly beautiful woman God created you to be?

What changes do you need to make in order to do that?

Prayer

Dear Jesus,

I pray to be filled with your love so that I can shed my layers of falseness and the need to fit in. Give me your strength to be the unique and beautiful woman you created me to be.

In Jesus' Name,

Amen

The next time you look at the woman in the mirror, take an inventory. Have you been denying your real self? Have you been covering up to fit in the traditional standard mode? You don't have to anymore. It's really your choice. God won't make you change. He invites all of us to change through the power of Christ, but He respects our right to choose.

As the woman in the mirror, you can choose today. You can choose to continue to slave away and see your reflection in the world's mirror, or you can make the better life-giving choice to see who you

THE WOMAN IN THE MIRROR

really are in the Mirror of God's Word. That Mirror says you are so finely crafted that the number of hairs on your head are counted, and that the only Son of God loved you so much He gave His life for you.

Now that's a story worth telling yourself every single day. That's the way to renew your mind. This world will continue to be relentless in its onslaught to sell us products, procedures, and promises to the fountain of youth. Again, what products and procedures you purchase are your choice. As long as you're spending within your budget and taking responsibility for your choices, it's all good. As for me, I'm a big fan of fashion, makeup, jewelry, and a wonderful designer named Mr. Clearance. I just refuse to let any of those things own me. I refuse, as a daughter of the King, to be solely defined by how the world looks at me on its scale of one to ten. Here are some differences between a daughter of the world and a daughter of the King:

Daughter of the World	Daughter of the King
Ranks herself on a 1-10 scale	Lives to honor her heavenly Father
Makes physical beauty her priority	Makes character her priority

Seeks approval/affirmation from others	Basks in the unconditional love and affirmation of her Heavenly Father
Looks at herself critically	Looks at herself through her Father's eyes of acceptance

Your reflection is just a mere glimpse of who you really are. As we take hold of our true value, we can move forth with a holy boldness to pursue our lives as an adventure ordered by Him. Through our words and with our examples, we can show our daughters, sisters, and nieces that we are wholly dedicated to our Father, and that we are beautiful because He made us. We belong to Him.

My prayer for you and me is that we'll join together in faith, lock arms, and as sisters in Christ, encourage, love, and honor one another. This battle with the mirror has been around forever, but so has God's plan. His plan is greater than any battle we face.

I believe that we are all born for such a time as this. We are born to show forth the praises of God without being hindered by self-esteem issues. No longer do we, or other women or girls, need to give ourselves away for someone's attention because we now know our value.

THE WOMAN IN THE MIRROR

God Doesn't Make Mistakes

We are the women in the mirror who know our worth, our value, and that we are not accidents or mistakes. Sonya Slaton, wife, mom, and pastor, joins our conversation now.

Let's listen as Sonya Slaton shares her heart with us:

> No matter what I was doing or what was going on in my life, the voice inside my head told me that I was a mistake. I felt I was a mistake because I was born to an unwed fourteen-year-old girl with an eighth-grade education. My father, whom I seldom saw, was only sixteen years old. I concluded at a very early age that since they had not planned me, I must be a mistake, and therefore my entire existence was a mistake. My mother never told me I was unwanted, and she did the best she could to raise me, and though my father never once uttered those words, his absence told me I was unwanted. For years, I struggled with being raised by a single mother, being poor, and literally despising everything about myself.

When it came to looking at my reflection in the mirror, I didn't like what I saw. I hated my hair, skin and nose. My hair wasn't straight or long enough. I thought my skin was too dark. Most of all I hated my nose. I remember staring at it for hours, pinching it, flattening it, trying to imagine how I would look if my nose was smaller. I remember thinking my sister's nose was little and cute. Why couldn't I have her nose? I dreamed that one day I would be rich and could afford plastic surgery. I literally hated everything about myself. I went to a very dark place and struggled with depression and thoughts of suicide. All of this stemmed from self - hate. I kept thinking if I was mistake and unwanted then nothing about me could be right.

When I was born again, everything changed. For the first time in my life, I felt unconditional love, and I thought that maybe I was worthwhile and good enough. John 3:16 told me that "God so loved this world that He gave His only begotten son." That included me!

However, everything changed when I read:

Jeremiah 1:5 (AMP)

Before I formed you in the womb I knew (and) approved of you.

This told me that God knew me before I was formed in my mother's womb. This meant that He had thought about me, and He had planned me. This revelation helped silence that awful condemning voice that told me my parents didn't plan or want me.

Slowly, I began to accept who I was and how God made me. I no longer dreamed of having plastic surgery to get the perfect nose. I stopped hating my hair. Okay, maybe I still have some bad hair days every now and then but I don't hate myself anymore. Receiving the love of God made me see myself differently. I now saw myself as a child of God, created in His image and likeness. How could I hate what He created? I realized He planned and created me. Wow, what a revelation: I'm not a mistake because God doesn't make mistakes.

As I read Sonya's story about her childhood, I think many of us hear what is said to us, but we also hear what is left unsaid. We fill in the blanks and connect the dots from "feeling like a mistake or unwanted" to sensing rejection based on our looks. The challenge for every woman in the mirror is to realize that God doesn't make mistakes.

He has made it plain and clear that we are His handiwork, His Masterpieces. We are His chosen treasures. We are uniquely designed and made in

His image. We cannot afford to connect the dots in our lives without giving first priority to what God has clearly spoken. God doesn't make mistakes. He formed us and approved of us from the time we were in our mother's womb.

This makes our mirror time very different. Now when we stand in front of the mirror, it's not about competing with others, or feeling disgusted by what we see or think we see. Our mirror time is about being a good steward of the life God has given us. Fixing our hair and putting on makeup is similar to brushing and flossing our teeth. It's good for us. We benefit from the mirror, but it is not an idol in our life. It's an enhancement—not an obsession.

This issue of our beauty and value is a choice. We can choose the world or we can choose what God says. We can continue to chase fleeting beauty and the fountain of youth, or we can stop the madness and accept God's Word as our absolute truth, and His Word is the absolute truth.

We are made in His image. Christ gives us everything we need to reflect His nature. The most beautiful women are the ones who love and obey God's Word above everything else. The world measures beauty by outward appearance, but God measures beauty by inner character.

The choice is ours. We can continue living in a perpetual state of comparing ourselves to the world's

THE WOMAN IN THE MIRROR

standards, or we can exchange that lie for God's truth. My prayer is that we will all accept His truth and reject the lie. As we do this, we will reap the benefits, and so will our sisters, friends, daughters, granddaughters, and generations to come.

As you lay down the mirror of the world and its expectations and pick up the Mirror of God's Word, remember the following truths:

You are meant for *more*.

You are *not* an accident.

Bask in His unconditional love and acceptance.

Be the *real* you.

God *doesn't* make mistakes.

God uniquely bestowed women with the ability to have a pure and quiet spirit. He gave us softer skin and nurturing spirits to love deeply and impact this world for His glory. Let's not trade that for momentary vanity or a number on a scale. If we know Jesus Christ as Lord and Savior, we are Daughters of the King. That, my dear sisters, changes absolutely everything.

Go ahead and look at the woman in the mirror. Tell her how beautiful God made her. Reject every lie for His truth. Ask Him to fill you with His spirit so you can fulfill His plan for your life. Tell everyone you know about the wonderful things Jesus has done in your life. Don't let fear hold you back. Get out there and live. You are God's girl, and you have been made with a plan and purpose. Quit putting life off, and get out there and live, laugh, enjoy, and share Jesus with everybody you meet.

Ephesians 2:10-11 (NLT)

For we are God's masterpiece. He has created us anew in Christ Jesus, so we can do the good things he planned for us long ago.

How can you know for sure that Jesus Christ is your Lord and Savior?

To know God and be ready for heaven, follow these steps:

A. Admit you are a sinner.

"There is no one righteous, not even one...for all have sinned and fall short of the glory of God" (Romans 3:10:23). (See Romans 5:8 and 6:23.)

Ask God's forgiveness.

"Everyone who calls on the name of the Lord will be saved" (Romans 10:13).

B. Believe in Jesus.

Put your trust in Him as your only hope of salvation.

"For God so loved the world that he gave his one and only Son, that whoever believes in him shall not perish but have eternal life" (John 3:16). (See John 14:6.)

Become a child of God by receiving Christ.

"To all who receive him, to those who believed in his name, he gave the right to become children of God" (John 1:12). (See Revelation 3:20.)

C. Confess that Jesus is your Lord.

"If you confess with your mouth, 'Jesus is Lord,' and believe in your heart that God raised him from the dead, you will be saved" (Romans 10:9). (See verse 10.)

If you'd like prayer or more information on the commitment you have just made, please visit http://monicaspeaks.com/contact/

Made in the USA
Charleston, SC
19 August 2013